A Scholarship Vocabulary Program

COURSE I

HAROLD LEVINE
Chairman Emeritus of English,
Benjamin Cardozo High School, New York

NORMAN LEVINE
Associate Professor of English,
City College of the City University of New York

ROBERT T. LEVINE
Professor of English,
North Carolina A & T State University

AMSCO

AMSCO SCHOOL PUBLICATIONS, INC.
315 Hudson Street / New York, N.Y. 10013

Vocabulary books by the authors

Vocabulary and Composition Through Pleasurable Reading,
Books I–VI
Vocabulary for Enjoyment, Books I–III
Vocabulary for the High School Student, Books A, B
Vocabulary for the High School Student
Vocabulary for the College-Bound Student
The Joy of Vocabulary
A Scholarship Vocabulary Program, Courses I–III

Please visit our Web site at:

www.amscopub.com

When ordering this book, please specify
either **R 611 S** or A SCHOLARSHIP VOCABULARY PROGRAM, COURSE I

ISBN 1-56765-020-1
NYC Item 56765-020-0

Printed in the United States of America
15 16 17 18 19   09 08 07 06 05 04

To the Student

A Scholarship Vocabulary Program, Course I teaches not only words but skills—especially the skills of close reading, critical thinking, and concise writing.

Every time you meet a lesson word in this book, you will be called upon to complete a sentence—not with the lesson word but with some other missing word. This, though you may not think so at first, requires close reading and critical thinking. Try to do what you are asked to do on page 1, and see if you don't agree. Then, for an example of a different way in which the book teaches these same skills, see page 38.

Concise writing is still another skill you will be learning in every lesson in this vocabulary book. The fastest way to learn what this skill is about is to turn now to the first concise writing exercise on page 8.

By the time you finish the book, you will have had hundreds of opportunities to perfect your reading, writing, and thinking skills—and you also will have learned many hundreds of useful words that belong in a well-educated person's vocabulary. Take a minute now to skim the Vocabulary Index, pages 132–138.

You will find ample provision for review within each regular lesson. Note, too, that every fifth lesson is a review of the previous four lessons.

Analogy questions have been included at the end of each regular lesson, in part, because they help with the review of lesson words and their synonyms, but more importantly because they stimulate critical thinking, a principal concern of this book.

The Authors

Contents

LESSON 1

alert (*adj.*) wide-awake and ready to act quickly; **watchful**;
ə-'lərt   **vigilant**

   1. Be *alert*; remove the pot from the stove (after, before)

     before _____ it boils over.

brawny (*adj.*) having well-developed muscles; **muscular**;
'brȯ-nē   **strong; sinewy**

   2. Weight (lifters, watchers) __lifters__ develop
     brawny shoulders.

candid (*adj.*) open and honest in what one says or does; **frank**;
'kan-dəd   **outspoken**

   3. *Candid* people tell the truth (except, even) __even__
     when it hurts.

chide (*v.*) express mild disapproval of; **scold**; **reprove**;
'chīd   **reproach**

   4. We use (gentle, harsh) __gentle__ tones when we
     chide someone.

counterfeit (*adj.*) made to resemble something genuine with in-
'kaunt-ər-ˌfit   tent to deceive; **forged**; **bogus**; **sham**

   5. I was (heartbroken, pretending) __pretending__;
     I shed *counterfeit* tears.

culprit (*n.*) person guilty of any offense or crime; **offender**;
'kəl-ˌprit   **malefactor**

   6. Don't (accuse, trust) __accuse__ her; she is not the *culprit*.

1

defraud (*v.*) deprive (someone) of something by deception or
di-'frŏd   fraud; **cheat**; **bilk**

> 7. If you were paid in (genuine, bogus) _bogus_ money,
> you were *defrauded*.

flaw (*n.*) something faulty or missing; **defect**; **imperfection**;
'flŏ   **blemish**

> 8. (Selfishness, Poverty) _Selfishness_ is a serious
> character *flaw*.

goad (*v.*) prod, as with a pointed stick; **spur**; **urge**; **incite**; **impel**
'gŏd

> 9. I quit (willingly, unwillingly) _unwillingly_; no
> one *goaded* me to do it.

maul (*v.*) handle roughly; injure by beating; **batter**; **mangle**
'mŏl

> 10. The child's new doll was *mauled* by her (jealous, gentle)
> _jealous_ playmates.

SENTENCE COMPLETION 1–10: Enter the required lesson words, as in 1, below.

---

1. The defendants _defraud_ed people of millions of dollars by printing and circulating _counterfeit_ bills.

2. If you had been more _alert_, you would have noticed the _flaw_ in the merchandise before purchasing it.

3. At first, he was not ~~candid~~ with us, but by gentle urging, and appealing to his better nature, we _goad_ed him into telling the truth.

4. The _____brawny_____ champion _____maul_____ed the

challenger so badly that the referee had to stop the bout.

5. Since the _____Culprit_____s had committed a serious offense,

they should have been punished, instead of just being

_____chid*_____ed.

SYNONYM ROUNDUP 1–10: Each completed line should have three synonyms. Enter the missing letters, as in 1, below.

---

1. b **a** tter   m **a** ngle   m **a** **u** l

2. ch __ __ t   defr __ __ d   b __ lk

3. d __ fect   __ __ perfection   fl __ w

4. fr __ nk   __ __ __ spoken   c __ nd __ d

5. m __ sc __ lar   br __ __ ny   s __ n __ wy

6. c __ lpr __ t   mal __ factor   offend __ r

7. g __ __ d   inc __ te   pr __ d

8. sc __ ld   repr __ ve   __ hide

9. sh __ m   b __ g __ s   counterf __ __ t

10. watch __ __ __   v __ g __ l __ nt   al __ rt

LESSON WORDS 11–20: Pronounce the word, spell it, study its meanings, and finish the sentence that follows it.

neglect (*v.*) give little or no attention to; **disregard**; **ignore**
ni-'glekt

    11. A *neglected* room looks (untidy, neat) ___untidy___

novice (*n.*) person new at something; **beginner**; **apprentice**;
'näv-əs   **neophyte; tyro**

    12. It is (rare, normal) ___normal___ for *novices* to make mistakes.

obstinate (*adj.*) unyielding; unreasonably determined to have
'äb-stə-nət   one's way; **stubborn**; **intransigent**

    13. *Obstinate* people (seldom, often) ___seldom___ change their views.

peer (*n.*) person of the same standing or ability as another; **equal**;
'pi(ə)r   **match**

    14. Pat is Jim's *peer* in tennis, but in other sports there is (little, considerable) ___considerable___ difference between them.

proficient (*adj.*) highly competent; **skilled**; **adept**
prə-'fish-ənt

    15. Chris is *proficient* with a needle, but I (can, can't) ___can't___ sew.

prohibit (*v.*) forbid by law or order; **ban**; **outlaw**; **interdict**
prō-'hib-ət

    16. Selling (soft, alcoholic) ___alcoholic___ drinks to children is *prohibited*.

sleuth (*n.*) one who follows a track or clue; **bloodhound**; **detec-**
'slüth   **tive**; **investigator**

    17. The arrests were made by *sleuths* posing as (addicts, police) ___police___.

truce (*n.*) temporary cessation of fighting; **cease-fire**; **armistice**
'trüs

18. Casualties went (up, down) _down_ considerably during the *truce*.

wan (*adj.*) pale, as from sickness or anxiety; **ashen**; **pallid**
'wän

19. You look *wan*. Is something (amusing, worrying) _worrying_ you?

wrath (*n.*) intense anger; resentful indignation; **ire**; **rage**; **fury**
'rath

20. (Wise, Quick) _wise_ decisions are rarely made in moments of *wrath*.

E **SENTENCE COMPLETION 11–20:** Enter the required lesson words from D, above.

1. Both sides are _obstinate_ _prohibited_ _ed_ from moving reinforcements into the battle zone during the _truce_.

2. As a(n) _sleuth_, Sherlock Holmes was in a class by himself; he had no _peers_.

3. _novice_ s in carpentry are not expected to be _proficient_ with tools.

4. Her friend has been _neglect_ ing his health; he looks _wan_.

5. Their _prohibit_ _obstinate_ refusal to compromise has aroused our _wrath_.

SYNONYM ROUNDUP 11–20: Each line, when completed, should have three words similar in meaning. Fill in the missing letters.

11. w __ n	pall __ d	ash __ n
12. b __ n	__ __ __ __ __ dict	proh __ b __ t
13. c __ __ se-fire	tr __ ce	arm __ sti __ e
14. __ __ __ regard	__ gn __ re	__ __ glect
15. eq __ __ l	m __ tch	p __ __ r
16. f __ ry	__ re	__ rath
17. investigat __ r	sl __ __ th	d __ t __ ctive
18. neoph __ te	t __ ro	n __ v __ ce
19. skil __ __ d	ad __ pt	profic __ __ nt
20. obst __ n __ te	intrans __ g __ nt	st __ bb __ rn

SYNONYMS: To avoid repetition, replace the boldfaced word or expression with a synonym from the vocabulary list below. See 1, below.

batter	**malefactor**	**bilk**	**vigilant**	**tyro**
armistice	**defect**	**intransigent**	**adept**	**reproach**

1. The fighting ceased when the **cease-fire** was agreed to.

1. ___armistice___

2. She was **unyielding**; she wouldn't yield an inch.

2. _____

3. We were in a state of alertness; everyone was told to be **alert**.

3. _____

4. Who is the **offender** who committed these offenses?

4. _____

5. Sometimes a **beginner** does well from the very beginning.

6. Those thugs are rough; they **rough up** their victims.

7. He lacks proficiency in typing; he is not so **proficient** as you.

8. She lifted a chiding finger, as if to **chide** us.

9. Don't let those frauds **defraud** you.

10. The gloves marked "imperfect" have a slight **imperfection**.

5. _____

6. _____

7. _____

8. _____

9. _____

10. _____

ANTONYMS: In the blank space in each sentence below, enter the word most nearly the antonym of the boldfaced word or words. Choose your antonyms from the following list. See 1, below.

adept	sinewy	bogus	ignore	outspoken
ban	stubborn	neophyte	ashen	reprove

1. Every **veteran** in golf was once a(n) ___neophyte___.

2. We **commend** those who excel and _____ those who loaf.

3. An expert can distinguish a(n) _____ diamond from a **genuine** one.

4. Many **give a great deal of attention** to TV but _____ their studies.

5. The rules _____ campfires but **permit** hiking.

6. The _____ stranger helped **frail** fellow passengers with their luggage.

7. Doesn't a(n) _____ employee deserve more pay than an **incompetent** one?

8. Most were **easy to persuade**, but one _____ member refused to cooperate.

9. They are usually _____, but this time they were **not candid** with us.

10. The patient who was _____ a week ago now looks much more **healthy**.

 CONCISE WRITING: Express the thought of each sentence in NO MORE THAN FOUR WORDS. See 1, below.

1. The people who lived next door to us were unreasonably determined to have their own way.

   Our neighbors were obstinate.

2. We paid too little attention to the employees who were new to the job.

   _____

3. The mechanic that she has been using is highly competent.

   _____

4. Not too many people in this wide world are open and honest in what they say and do.

   _____

5. He had the pale look of someone who is ill or extremely worried about something.

   _____

6. It is essential for guards to be watchful and ready to act quickly.

   _____

7. You are a person of the same ability as myself.

   _____

8. The smoking of cigarettes or cigars is forbidden by law in this building.

   _____

ANALOGIES: Which lettered pair of words—**a, b, c, d,** or **e**—most nearly has the same relationship as the numbered pair? Enter the letter of your answer in the space provided. The first analogy question has been answered and explained as a sample.

1. BOGUS : GENUINE

   a. spacious : roomy
   c. careful : cautious
   e. precious : valuable

   b. grateful : thankful
   d. defective : perfect

   1. ___*d*___

   Explanation: BOGUS and GENUINE are antonyms. The only lettered pair that consists of antonyms is **defective** and **perfect**.

2. BILK : DEFRAUD

   a. conceal : disclose
   c. ask : inquire
   e. begin : end

   b. assist : hinder
   d. dissent : agree

   2. _____

3. NEOPHYTE : EXPERIENCE

   a. tyrant : pity
   c. believer : faith
   e. executive : power

   b. celebrity : fame
   d. expert : skill

   3. _____

   Hint: a NEOPHYTE lacks EXPERIENCE.

4. BRAWNY : STRENGTH

   a. penniless : money
   c. ignorant : knowledge
   e. enraged : wrath

   b. busy : time
   d. weary : energy

   4. _____

5. INTRANSIGENT : YIELD

   a. generous : share
   c. reasonable : compromise
   e. intelligent : learn

   b. cooperative : help
   d. impatient : wait

   5. _____

   Hint: an INTRANSIGENT person does not YIELD.

6. CRACK : DEFECT

    a. dime : coin   *b.* apple : core

    c. branch : tree   *d.* bone : fracture

    e. rose : thorn   6. _____

7. FLAWLESS : BLEMISH

    a. tasty : flavor   *b.* spacious : room

    c. priceless : value   *d.* stale : freshness

    e. perilous : danger   7. _____

LESSON 2

A **LESSON WORDS 1–10:** Pronounce the word, spell it, study its meanings, and finish the sentence that follows it. See 1, below.

antagonistic (*adj.*)   showing opposition or ill will; **opposed**; **hos-**
an-ˌtag-ə-ˈnis-tik   **tile**; **inimical**

1. My (friends, foes) ___**friends**___ were unexpectedly *antagonistic* to my idea.

botch (*v.*)   do clumsily; spoil by poor work; foul up; **bungle**; **ruin**
ˈbäch

2. A (careful, careless) ___careless___ mechanic *botched* the repair job.

dearth (*n.*)   inadequate supply; **scarcity**; **lack**
ˈdərth

3. Homes were (easy, hard) ___hard___ to find; there was a *dearth* of housing.

dire (*adj.*)   arousing dread or deep distress; **dreadful**; **ominous**; ˈdī(ə)r   **threatening**

4. We heard the *dire* forecast of the (end, spread) ___end___ of democracy.

dolt (*n.*)   dull, stupid person; **dunce**; **oaf**; **clod**; **blockhead**
ˈdōlt

5. When I forget my (keys, fears) ___keys___ , I feel like a *dolt*.

fraught (*adj.*)   full of (followed by *with*); **filled**; **laden**; **charged**
ˈfròt

6. (Familiar, New) ___New___ ventures are often *fraught* with surprises.

glut (n.) supply that exceeds demand; **oversupply**; **surplus**;
'glət   **superabundance**

> 7. Dealers (enjoy, dislike) _enjoy_ having a *glut*
> of new merchandise.

humane (adj.) full of sympathy and consideration for others and
yü-'mān   for animals; **charitable**; **altruistic**

> 8. *Humane* people try to (ease, ignore) _ease_ the suf-
> fering of others.

intrude (v.) thrust oneself without invitation; **encroach**; **tres-**
in-'trüd   **pass**

> 9. It is very rude to *intrude* in a (private, public) _private_
> discussion.

loath (adj.) strongly disinclined; **unwilling**; **reluctant**; **hesi-**
'lōth   **tant**

> 10. People are *loath* to part with something they (dislike, need)
> _dislike_ .

 SENTENCE COMPLETION 1–10: Enter the required lesson
 words.

---

1. Everyone was _antagonistic_ to the hungry ex-

convict, except one _humane_ bishop, who invited him to

dinner and gave him a lodging for the night.

2. I felt like a(n) _dolt_ when I _botch_ed a

simple arithmetic problem.

3. Holmes was _fraught_ to ask Watson to join him on the

mission because it was _loath_ with danger.

4. When there was a(n) _dearth_ of tomatoes, they were $3.00 a pound; now that there is a(n) _glut_ of tomatoes, they are three pounds for $1.00.

5. Ignoring _dire_ warnings from the townspeople, the hero and heroine went ahead with their plan to _intrude_ on Count Dracula's privacy.

SYNONYM ROUNDUP 1–10: Each completed line should have three synonyms. Enter the missing letters, as in 1, below.

---

1. ant **a** g **o** nistic   in **i** mical   **o** **p** posed

2. b __ ngle   ru __ n   b __ tch

3. d __ re   thr __ __ tening   __ minous

4. hum __ ne   altr __ istic   char __ t __ ble

5. l __ den   ch __ rged   fr __ __ ght

6. o __ f   cl __ d   d __ lt

7. rel __ ct __ nt   h __ sit __ nt   __ oath

8. scar __ ity   dear __ __   l __ ck

9. s __ rpl __ s   __ __ __ __ __ supply gl __ t

10. tr __ sp __ ss   __ __ trude   encr __ __ ch

LESSON WORDS 11–20: Pronounce the word, spell it, study its meanings, and finish the sentence that follows it.

---

novelty (*n.*)   something new; **newness**; **change**; **innovation**
ˈnäv-əl-tē

    11. A (heat, cold) _heat_ wave at the North Pole would
        be a *novelty*.

parch (*v.*)   make dry with heat; **dry**; **scorch**; **dehydrate**
ˈpärch

    12. The summer (drought, hurricane) _drought_
        parched the landscape.

rue (*v.*)   wish undone; feel remorse for; **regret**; **deplore**
ˈrü

    13. If you act (cautiously, hastily) _hastily_, you
        may *rue* the outcome.

sparse (*adj.*)   thinly scattered; not dense; **meager**; **scanty**
ˈspärs

    14. A (losing, winning) _losing_ team usually draws
        sparse crowds.

teem (*v.*)   be abundant; **abound**; **swarm**
ˈtēm

    15. In (summer, winter) _summer_, the beaches *teem*
        with bathers.

tractable (*adj.*)   easy to manage or control; **compliant**; **docile**;
ˈtrak-tə-bəl   **obedient**

    16. *Tractable* pupils do not (disregard, heed) _disregard_
        instructions.

trite (*adj.*)   so overused as no longer to have interest, freshness, or
ˈtrīt   originality; **commonplace**; **stale**; **timeworn**

    17. A creative writer tries to (avoid, use) _avoid_ trite
        expressions.

unruly (*adj.*)   resistant to discipline or control; **ungovernable**;
ˌən-ˈrü-lē   **recalcitrant**

    18. A (dull, fascinating) _dull_ program may
        make an audience *unruly*.

wharf (n.) structure where ships load and unload; **dock**; **pier**
'wórf

19. The (limousine, yacht) __Yacht__ was tied up
along the *wharf*.

wilt (v.) lose, or cause to lose, freshness and become limp; **droop**;
'wilt   **wither**

20. The *wilting* plants sprang to life after the (rain, frost)
__rain__.

| E | **SENTENCE COMPLETION 11–20:** Enter the required les-
son words from D, above.

---

1. The garden __teem__s with destructive beetles when the
population of their natural enemies is __sparse__.

2. As the empty rowboat drifted from the shore, we
__rue__d our carelessness in not tying the boat firmly to
the __wharf__.

3. Max's dog Fido was so __unruly__ that he was sent to
obedience school for a month; since his return, he has been more
__tractable__.

4. There is not one bit of __novelty__ in that movie; every
idea, every situation, every word in it is __trite__.

5. August's dry heat __parch__ed the soil and
__wilt__ed the corn.

F   SYNONYM ROUNDUP 11–20: Enter the missing letters.

11. ab __ __ nd   sw __ rm   t __ __ m

12. com __ __ __ place   tr __ te   t __ meworn

13. __ __ __ pliant   d __ c __ le   __ __ actable

14. __ __ hydrate   sc __ rch   p __ rch

15. __ ue   depl __ re   r __ gr __ t

16. d __ ck   p __ __ r   __ __ arf

17. __ __ oop   w __ lt   w __ th __ r

18. in __ __ vation   __ __ __ ness   n __ v __ lty

19. m __ __ ger   sp __ __ se   scant __

20. ungov __ __ nable   recal __ __ trant   __ __ ruly

G   SYNONYMS: To avoid repetition, replace the boldfaced word or expression with a synonym from the vocabulary list below. See 1, below.

---

oaf	deplore	pier	wither	bungle
innovation	recalcitrant	inimical	altruistic	ominous

1. At what **dock** is the ship docked?

2. People want something new; they like **newness**.

3. The fresh-cut flowers are beginning to **lose freshness**.

4. A few of our old friends are now **unfriendly** to us.

5. I did not regret my part in the play, but I **regretted** my foolishness in turning down the leading role when it was offered.

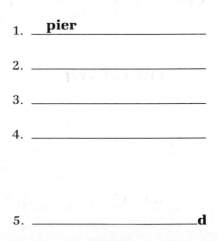

1. __pier__

2. _____

3. _____

4. _____

5. _____**d**

6. Most of the youngsters were fairly easy to control; only a few were **resistant to control**.

6. _____

7. Some individuals show no consideration for others; they are not **considerate**.

7. _____

8. The work may be **done clumsily** if entrusted to clumsy hands.

8. _____d

9. So **dreadful** were the first reports of the earthquake that we dreaded hearing any more about it.

9. _____

10. Though you are surely not a(an) **stupid person**, you showed unbelievable stupidity.

10. _____

ANTONYMS: In the blank space in each sentence below, enter the word most nearly the antonym of the boldfaced word or words. Choose your antonyms from the following list. See 1, below.

hesitant	**timeworn**	**clod**	**encroach**	**abound**
hostile	**meager**	**docile**	**charitable**	**superabundance**

1. This **congested** island formerly had a very __meager__ population.

2. Trespassers, **keep out**; do not _____ on this property.

3. There is no **dearth** of help; we have a(n) _____ of volunteers.

4. Did the casualties result from **friendly** or _____ gunfire?

5. You should abandon your **inhumane** attitude and try to be

_____ .

6. Though a few are _____, most are **willing** to participate.

7. If opportunities **are scarce** here, seek a place where they

_____ .

8. A(n) _____ expression should be replaced with something **original**.

9. Even an **intelligent person** can sometimes behave like a(n)

_____ .

10. What makes a(n) _____ child suddenly become **disobedient**?

CONCISE WRITING: Express the thought of each sentence in NO MORE THAN FOUR WORDS, as in 1, below.

---

1. The ideas that he is proposing are not new, but have been heard time and time again in the past.

   His ideas are trite.

---

2. These flowers are losing their freshness and are becoming limp.

_____

3. We wish the mistakes that we have made were undone.

_____

4. Shouldn't everyone have sympathy and consideration for other human beings?

_____

5. The pupils that she has been teaching are not difficult to manage.

_____

6. The management expels those who have the nerve to come to share in the festivities without being invited.

_____

ANALOGIES: Which lettered pair of words—**a, b, c, d, or e**—most nearly has the same relationship as the numbered pair? Enter the letter of your answer in the space provided.

1. DOLT : BRAINPOWER

    a. ruler : authority   *b.* child : maturity
    c. parent : responsibility   *d.* graduate : diploma
    e. giant : brawn   1. _____

2. ENEMY : INIMICAL

    a. prisoner : free   *b.* chatterbox : quiet
    c. artisan : clumsy   *d.* tyro : inexperienced
    e. ally : hostile   2. _____

3. SPARSE : DENSE

    a. scarce : abundant   *b.* wan : pale
    c. loath : unwilling   *d.* priceless : valuable
    e. later : subsequent   3. _____

4. GLUT : PRICES

    a. argument : tempers   *b.* cloudburst : streams
    c. cold front : temperatures   *d.* fire : smoke
    e. encouragement : hopes   4. _____

5. ANTAGONISM : COMPROMISE

    a. advertising : sales   *b.* goodwill : peace
    c. irrigation : crops   *d.* sleet : transportation
    e. practice : improvement   5. _____

    Hint: ANTAGONISM interferes with COMPROMISE.

6. ALTRUISTIC : SHARE

    a. embittered : forgive   *b.* recalcitrant : obey
    c. disobliging : cooperate   *d.* undecided : act
    e. grateful : appreciate   6. _____

7. BUNGLER : PROFICIENT

    a. complainer : dissatisfied   *b.* busybody : meddlesome
    c. accomplice : blameless   *d.* celebrity : famous
    e. liar : untrustworthy   7. _____

LESSON 3

LESSON WORDS 1–10: Pronounce the word, spell it, study its meanings, and finish the sentence that follows it.

---

abate (*v.*) diminish in force or intensity; let up; **moderate**; **subside**
ə-'bāt

1. We took shelter (after, until) _____until_____ the storm *abated*.

cower (*v.*) crouch in fear from something that threatens; **cringe**; **quail**
'kaü(-ə)r

2. A (bully, clown) _____bully_____ enjoys making others *cower*.

crest (*n.*) highest part; **top**; **summit**
'krest

3. Heavy trucks (lose, gain) _____lose_____ speed approaching the *crest* of a road.

devise (*v.*) make up; **concoct**; **formulate**; **design**
di-'vīz

4. (Troops, Commanders) _____troops_____ generally do not *devise* battle plans.

din (*n.*) steady loud noise; **uproar**; **racket**; **tumult**
'din

5. A rumbling *din* accompanied the (fashion, fireworks) _____fireworks_____ display.

entreat (*v.*) ask earnestly; plead with; **beg**; **beseech**; **implore**; **importune**
in-'trēt

6. We wanted to leave, but they *entreated* us to (go, stay) _____stay_____ .

feasible (*adj.*) capable of being done; **doable**; **possible**; **practic-**
'fē-zə-bəl   **able**; **viable**

> 7. Before (1776, 1492) ___1492___, a transatlantic voyage
>   was not deemed *feasible*.

groundless (*adj.*) without foundation; uncalled for; **baseless**;
'graun-(d)ləs   **gratuitous**

> 8. Joe is (fine, ill) ___fine___; your fears about his health
>   are *groundless*.

horde (*n.*) large, moving crowd; **multitude**; **throng**; **mob**
'hȯ(ə)rd

> 9. Merchants are (happy, unhappy) ___happy___ when
>   *hordes* of tourists arrive.

loom (*v.*) come into view indistinctly; take shape; **appear**;
'lüm   **emerge**

> 10. A battle *looms* whenever old (friends, foes) ___foes___
>   cross paths.

SENTENCE COMPLETION 1–10: Enter the required lesson words.

---

1. When the horrid bulk of a dragon ___loom___s at the cave's
   entrance, even the bravest knights ___cower___.

2. Looking down from the hill's ___crest___, Don Quixote
   claimed to see a(n) ___horde___ of armed foes, but his squire
   Sancho Panza saw only a cloud of dust.

3. The attorney ___entreat___ed the jury to ignore the
   ___groundless___ accusations that had been leveled
   against her client.

4. Randy thought the plan that the committee had
_____ *devise* d would not work, but most of the other members believed it to be _____ *feasible* .

5. I hope that _____ *din* that is interfering with our conversation
will soon _____ *abate* .

 SYNONYM ROUNDUP 1–10: Each completed line should have three synonyms. Enter the missing letters.

---

1. app __ __ r	__ merge	l __ __ m
2. b __ s __ less	ground __ __ __ __	grat __ __ tous
3. cr __ nge	qu __ __ l	c __ w __ r
4. desi __ n	form __ late	__ __ vise
5. d __ n	upr __ __ r	r __ ck __ t
6. __ __ treat	impl __ re	__ __ portune
7. m __ d __ rate	s __ bs __ de	__ bate
8. pract __ c __ ble	f __ __ sible	vi __ ble
9. s __ mm __ t	t __ p	__ rest
10. thr __ ng	h __ rde	m __ lt __ tude

 LESSON WORDS 11–20: Pronounce the word, spell it, study its meanings, and finish the sentence that follows it.

---

patron (*n.*) regular customer; **client**; **supporter**
ˈpā-trən

11. A business may (fail, prosper) _____ *fail* if it dis-
pleases its *patrons.*

persist (*v.*) go on despite difficulty; refuse to give up; **persevere**;
pər-'sist   **continue**

12. Some (heed, ignore) _ignore_ all warnings and *persist* in smoking.

prone (*adj.*) having a natural bent or tendency; **inclined**; **disposed**; **apt**
'prōn

13. A person who is (seldom, often) _often_ wrong may be *prone* to error.

prudent (*adj.*) showing sound judgment; **sensible**; **wise**; **judicious**; **discreet**
'prüd-ᵊnt

14. It is *prudent* to (close, lock) _lock_ all doors before leaving home.

rouse (*v.*) bring out of a state of inactivity; **wake**; **stir**; **excite**; **provoke**
'raŭz

15. The (stillness, doorbell) _doorbell_ *roused* me from my daydream.

scoff (*v.*) show scornful disapproval; **sneer**; **jeer**; **gibe**
'skäf

16. People *scoff* at those who claim to know (everything, little) _everything_.

sham (*n.*) something not what it is supposed to be; **hoax**; **fake**
'sham

17. If he was (able, forbidden) _forbidden_ to testify, his trial was a *sham*.

spurn (*v.*) reject disdainfully; turn down; **decline**; **refuse**; **scorn**
'spərn

18. Workers *spurn* contracts that (reduce, raise) _reduce_ their earnings.

timid (*adj.*) easily frightened; **afraid**; **timorous**; **shy**
'tim-əd

19. *Timid* individuals are (disinclined, prone) _disinclined_ to complain.

unkempt (*adj.*) not neat or orderly; **uncombed; disheveled;**
,ən-'kem(p)t **untidy; slovenly**

20. We are (unlikely, disposed) _____ to be
unkempt when we first awake.

SENTENCE COMPLETION 11–20: Enter the required lesson words from D, above.

---

1. A snake approaching a nest can ___*rouse*___ a normally
___*timid*___ bird to attack fiercely.

2. Though the people in town ___*scoff*___ed at the idea of a
flying machine, the Wright brothers ___*persist*___ed until
their airplane worked.

3. Since my brother believed Rita was ___*prone*___ to accidents,
he graciously offered to do some or all of the driving, but she
___*spurn*___ed the offer.

4. Kenny is usually ___*unkempt*___, but he realizes it is
___*prudent*___ to comb his hair before going to be interviewed for a job.

5. A store whose so-called "sales" are a(n) ___*sham*___
cannot count on me as one of its ___*patron*___s.

SYNONYM ROUNDUP 11–20: Each line, when completed, should have three words similar in meaning. Fill in the missing letters.

11. __ pt	disp __ sed	pr __ ne
12. cli __ nt	s __ pp __ rter	p __ tr __ n
13. ref __ se	d __ cl __ ne	sp __ rn
14. dish __ v __ led	unk __ __ pt	sl __ v __ nly
15. continu __	p __ rs __ st	pers __ v __ re
16. f __ ke	sh __ m	h __ __ x
17. j __ __ r	__ neer	__ __ off
18. sens __ ble	discr __ __ t	__ rude __ __
19. t __ m __ d	sh __	tim __ r __ __ s
20. w __ ke	st __ r	r __ __ se

G **SYNONYMS:** To avoid repetition, replace the boldfaced word or expression with a synonym from the vocabulary list below.

---

multitude	**viable**	**judicious**	**subside**	**concoct**
baseless	**quail**	**decline**	**implore**	**disheveled**

1. Even when you comb unruly hair, it may look **uncombed**.

1. _____

2. The rain has not let up; we can't leave until it **lets up**.

2. _____ **s**

3. If your plan is **practicable**, we will put it into practice.

3. _____

4. They **pleaded with** us to wait, but we ignored their plea.

4. _____ **d**

5. Are there grounds for worry, or are your fears **groundless**?

5. _____

6. I am sure you have the sense to make a **sensible** choice.

6. _____

7. Their refusal surprises me; they have never **refused** our help.

7. _____ **d**

8. The place was crowded; it was hard to find anyone in that **crowd**.

8. _____

9. When danger looms, act quickly; don't **cower** like a coward.

9. _____

10. Someone has just **devised** a new device to combat auto theft.

10. _____**ed**

 ANTONYMS: In the blank space in each sentence below, enter the word most nearly the antonym of the boldfaced word or words. Choose your antonyms from the following list.

---

tumult	**discreet**	**moderate**	**summit**	**persevere**
untidy	**doable**	**timorous**	**emerge**	**scorn**

1. As soon as one problem **disappears**, another _____**s** on the horizon.

2. Most **give up** quickly, but a few _____ until they reach their goal.

3. There is no telling whether the storm will **intensify** or _____.

4. What seems _____ on paper may be **impossible** in practice.

5. How long did it take to get to the _____ of the hill from its **base**?

6. Today we reconsidered and **embraced** a plan that we had _____**ed** only yesterday.

7. The _____ of wailing sirens shattered the **stillness** of the night.

8. Everyone at the dance was **well groomed**; no one was _____.

9. Not all were **courageous**; a few were so _____ that they fled in panic.

10. Even _____ shoppers occasionally make an **unwise** purchase.

CONCISE WRITING: Express the thought of each sentence in NO MORE THAN FOUR WORDS.

1. Is the pain that he has been suffering from diminishing in intensity?

———————————————————————————

2. All of a sudden, the steady loud noise came to an end.

———————————————————————————

3. There is no foundation for the accusations that she has been making.

———————————————————————————

4. In all probability, I looked as if I had given little or no attention to my personal appearance.

———————————————————————————

5. Ahead, the mountains were coming into view in indistinct form.

———————————————————————————

6. What is it that made you refuse to give up?

———————————————————————————

ANALOGIES: Which lettered pair of words—**a, b, c, d,** or **e**—most nearly has the same relationship as the numbered pair? Enter the letter of your answer in the space provided.

1. DIN : NOISE

    a. melon : vegetable   *b.* tree : oak
    c. carbon monoxide : gas   *d.* potato : fruit
    e. fall : pain   1. ———

2. SPURN : DECLINE

    a. deplore : rue   *b.* complicate : simplify
    c. grant : withhold   *d.* dismiss : hire
    e. conserve : squander   2. ———

3. QUITTER : PERSIST

  a. pedestrian : walk   *b.* guide : conduct
  c. inspector : examine   *d.* guard : protect
  e. dissenter : agree   3. _____

4. FEASIBLE : DO

  a. inconspicuous : see   *b.* unalterable : change
  c. imitable : copy   *d.* obvious : conceal
  e. complex : understand   4. _____

5. ABATE : INTENSIFY

  a. bar : exclude   *b.* commend : reprove
  c. chide : scold   *d.* perceive : understand
  e. prohibit : ban   5. _____

6. CREST : WAVE

  a. mouth : river   *b.* dock : ship
  c. roof : building   *d.* rainbow : sky
  e. waste : haste   6. _____

7. SCOFF : DISAPPROVAL

  a. blush : embarrassment   *b.* compliment : displeasure
  c. yawn : interest   *d.* hesitate : confidence
  e. volunteer : unwillingness   7. _____

LESSON 4

 LESSON WORDS 1–10: Pronounce the word, spell it, study its meanings, and finish the sentence that follows it.

---

civil (*adj.*)   adequately polite; **mannerly**; **genteel**; **courteous**
ˈsiv-əl

   1. Avoid (foul, polite) _foul_ language; try to be more *civil*.

condense (*v.*)   reduce the extent of; express in fewer words; **com-**
kən-ˈden(t)s   **press**; **abridge**

   2. The *condensed* edition is (twice, half) _half_ the size of the original.

culpable (*adj.*)   deserving censure; **blameworthy**; **guilty**; **rep-**
ˈkəl-pə-bəl   **rehensible**

   3. If they are *culpable*, let us (condemn, praise) _condemn_ them.

delectable (*adj.*)   very pleasing; **delightful**; **delicious**; **luscious**
di-ˈlek-tə-bəl

   4. Some (like, dislike) _dislike_ bananas, but others find them *delectable*.

edible (*adj.*)   fit for eating; **eatable**; **comestible**
ˈed-ə-bəl

   5. The only *edible* part of a walnut is the (shell, kernel) _kernel_.

garrulous (*adj.*)   inclined to chatter to excess, especially about un-
ˈgar-ə-ləs   important matters; **talkative**; **loquacious**

   6. If you are *garrulous*, you will (bore, delight) _bore_ your audience.

gist (*n.*)   main point of a matter; **essence**; **core**; **pith**
ˈjist

    7. The *gist* of a news story is in its (headline, ending) __headline__.

insolent (*adj.*) boldly disrespectful; **insulting**; **impertinent**;
ˈin-s(ə-)lənt   **impudent**; **rude**

    8. Show (regard, contempt) ___regard___ for the court; don't be *insolent*.

irk (*v.*)   **annoy**; **irritate**; **disgust**; **exasperate**; **vex**
ˈərk

    9. It *irks* voters when legislators (observe, violate) ___violate___ the law.

knack (*n.*)   special skill for doing something; **gift**; **talent**; **flair**
ˈnak

    10. Troubleshooters have a *knack* for (solving, creating) ___creating___ problems.

SENTENCE COMPLETION 1–10: Enter the required lesson words.

---

1. Sheila is by nature ___garrulous___; whenever she tells a story, her friends plead with her to ___condense___ it.

2. Wouldn't it ___irk___ you if your entire class were punished for something that only one or two classmates were ___culpable___ of?

3. I didn't particularly enjoy the meal; the food was ___edible___ but not ___delectable___.

4. A good thinker has the ___Knack___ of getting quickly to the ___gist___ of a problem, without wasting time on lesser matters.

5. Umpires usually have enough self-control to be ___civil___ to a player who questions their judgment, even when that player is a bit ___insolent___.

SYNONYM ROUNDUP 1–10: Each completed line should have three synonyms. Enter the missing letters.

---

1. abri _d_ ge   c _o_ mpress   _con_ dense

2. blamew _o_ _c_ thy   reprehens _i_ ble   c _u_ lp _a_ ble

3. d _e_ l _i_ cious   _d_ _e_ lectable   lus c _i_ ous

4. ed _i_ ble   com _e_ stible   e _d_ t _a_ ble

5. ex _a_ sperate   v _e_ x   _i_ _r_ k

6. g _i_ ft   _k_ nack   t _a_ l _e_ nt

7. imp _e_ rtinent   _i_ _m_ pudent   ins _u_ l _a_ nt

8. gent _e_ _e_ l   c _o_ _u_ rt _e_ ous   c _i_ v _i_ l

9. _e_ _s_ sence   p _i_ th   g _i_ st

10. talk _a_ tive   loq _u_ _a_ cious   garr _u_ lous

LESSON WORDS 11–20: Pronounce the word, spell it, study its meanings, and finish the sentence that follows it.

---

literate (*adj.*)   able to read and write; **educated**; **cultured**
'lit-ə-rət

    11. (Nobody, Everyone) __Nobody__ has to be *literate* to watch TV.

mock (*v.*)   treat with scorn or contempt; **ridicule**; **taunt**; **deride**
'mäk

    12. Even my friends might *mock* me if I misspelled (*sinewy*, *cat*) __Cat__ .

obliging (*adj.*)   ready to do favors; **good-natured**; **amiable**;
ə-'blī-jiŋ   **accommodating**

    13. *Obliging* classmates (sharpen, use) __sharpen__ my pencils.

prevail (*v.*)   be victorious; become dominant; **triumph**; **predom-**
pri-'vā(ə)l   **inate**

    14. Unfortunately, (reason, ignorance) __reason__ sometimes *prevails*.

quell (*v.*)   put an end to; **suppress**; **crush**; **extinguish**
'kwel

    15. All is quiet; the (disturbance, peace) __disturbance__ has been *quelled*.

queue (*n.*)   line of people or vehicles waiting their turn; **file**; **line**
'kyü

    16. Shoppers on long *queues* tend to complain of the (prices, delay) __delay__ .

relish (*v.*)   take pleasure in; like the taste of; **savor**; **enjoy**; **like**
'rel-ish

    17. A (compliment, scolding) __scolding__ is something we do not *relish*.

resolution (*n.*)   firmness of purpose; **determination**; **resolve**
ˌrez-ə-'lü-shən

    18. His *resolution* to resist made it (hard, easy) __hard__ for us to prevail.

verge (*n.*)   point beyond which something happens; **edge**; **brink**;
'vərj   **threshold**

19. The (overfed, neglected) _____neglected_____ pets were
    on the *verge* of starvation.

whim (*n.*)   sudden odd idea or desire; passing notion; **fancy**; **ca-**
'wim   **price**

20. It is (risky, prudent) _____risky_____ to change course on
    the basis of a *whim*.

E   **SENTENCE COMPLETION 11–20:** Enter the required lesson words from D, above.

---

1. Ahead 6–0, the home team began to ____mock____ us, but that

   only strengthened our ~~whim~~ resolution to win the game.

2. The emperor was on the ____verge____ of ____quelling____ **ing**

   the uprising when his generals decided to join forces with the

   rebels.

3. In our country, the rule of law ____prevail____s, rather than

   the ~~(illegible)~~ whim of some dictator.

4. We do not ____relish____ getting on the end of a slow-moving

   ____queue____ when there is only one checkout counter.

5. The youngsters will enjoy the book, even though they are not

   yet ____literate____, if they can get ____obliging____

   adults to read them a story from it.

SYNONYM ROUNDUP 11–20: Each line, when completed, should have three words similar in meaning. Fill in the missing letter.

11. _e_ ile | l _i_ ne | qu _eu_ e

12. _en_ joy | r _eli_ sh | s _a_ v _o_ r

13. br _i_ nk | v _e_ rge | thresh _ol_ d

14. am _i_ able | ac _com_ modating | _o_ bliging

15. fan _c_ y | _w_ him | _ca_ price

16. c _ul_ t _u_ red | ed _u_ cated | l _i_ t _e_ rate

17. qu _e_ ll | s _u_ press | exting _ui_ sh

18. m _o_ ck | r _i_ d _i_ c _u_ le | _de_ ride

19. res _ol_ u tion | _de_ termination | _re_ solve

20. tr _iu_ mph | prev _ai_ l | _pre_ dominate

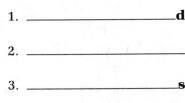

SYNONYMS: To avoid repetition, replace the boldfaced word with a synonym from the vocabulary list below.

loquacious   savor   genteel   flair   exasperate
impertinent reprehensible deride   resolve   comestible

1. She **ridiculed** me; she said everything I did was ridiculous.

1. _____ **d**

2. Don't blame us; we are not **blameworthy**.

2. _____

3. It **irritates** us to listen to irritating complaints.

3. _____ **s**

4. My brother is **courteous** to others, but he shows me no courtesy.

4. _____

5. Lori is determined; we cannot say she lacks **determination**.

5. _____

6. I didn't **like** the soup, but I liked the crispy breadsticks.

6. _____

7. She has a **talent** for acting, but I am not a talented performer.

7. _____

8. He is very **talkative**; he keeps talking and talking.

8. _____

9. When campers are hungry, they eat anything that is **eatable**.

9. _____

10. Joe is not **disrespectful**; he respects everyone.

10. _____

 ANTONYMS: Enter the word most nearly the antonym of the boldfaced word or words. Choose your antonyms from the following list.

---

suppress   core   garrulous   comestible   abridge
illiterate   vex   predominate   courteous   blameworthy

1. Skip the **unimportant details**; let's discuss the

   _____ of the problem.

2. You may very well be **guiltless**, but the others are

   clearly _____.

3. One cannot predict with certainty who will **lose** and who will

   _____.

4. A(n) _____ person with a secret cannot remain **close-mouthed** about it.

5. Chokecherries look _____, but they are **not fit to eat**.

6. That constant din apparently **did not irk** others, but it

   _____**ed** us.

7. His remarks are seldom _____; he has an **uncivil** tongue.

8. If we were _____, **educated** persons would have to read and write for us.

9. The rebellion was _____**ed,** and those who had **fomented** it fled.

10. I meant to **expand** my talk but had to _____ it for lack of time.

CONCISE WRITING: Express the thought of each sentence in NO MORE THAN FOUR WORDS.

---

1. The line of people who are waiting their turn keeps growing.

   _____

2. He is the sort of fellow who never does anyone a favor.

   _____

3. Grandma serves meals that are very pleasing to the taste.

   _____

4. The person who lives next door is inclined to talk too much about unimportant things.

   _____

5. Please express the motion that you are making in fewer words.

   _____

6. People who frequently go to the opera take pleasure in listening to the music that Puccini composed.

   _____

ANALOGIES: Which lettered pair of words—**a, b, c, d,** or **e**—most nearly has the same relationship as the numbered pair? Enter the letter of your answer in the space provided.

1. SCAPEGOAT : CULPABLE

    a. follower : loyal   *b.* enemy : inimical
    c. culprit : guilty   *d.* ignoramus : knowledgeable
    e. celebrity : popular

                             1. _____

2. RELISH : APPRECIATE

    a. scorn : entreat   *b.* devise : concoct
    c. tarry : hurry   *d.* reproach : congratulate
    e. seek : shun

                             2. _____

3. LITERACY : IGNORANCE

    a. inflammation : pain   *b.* uncertainty : anxiety
    c. overwork : fatigue   *d.* novelty : curiosity
    e. conservation : waste

                             3. _____

4. PERSISTENT : PREVAIL

    a. obstinate : yield   *b.* civil : offend
    c. disobliging : help   *d.* timid : retreat
    e. confident : hesitate

                             4. _____

5. COMESTIBLE : EAT

    a. vague : understand   *b.* unfeasible : accomplish
    c. flexible : bend   *d.* immortal : destroy
    e. urgent : postpone

                             5. _____

6. FOMENT : QUELL

    a. abridge : expand   *b.* subside : abate
    c. interdict : prohibit   *d.* teem : swarm
    e. provoke : rouse

                             6. _____

7. WAVERING : RESOLUTION

    a. adept : skill   *b.* despondent : hope
    c. prudent : judgment   *d.* loquacious : words
    e. energetic : vigor

                             7. _____

LESSON 5: REVIEW AND ENRICHMENT

 CLOSE READING: Read the following statements. Then answer questions 1–10.

STATEMENTS

Eliza's dog Marbles was amazingly obedient; the first time I saw him, I said "Roll over," and he did.

In selecting a crew for the *Hispaniola*, Squire Trelawney relied heavily on the advice of Long John Silver, a person he hardly knew.

Pocahontas begged her father, Powhatan, to spare John Smith's life.

After his expulsion from the Massachusetts Bay Colony, Roger Williams founded the colony of Rhode Island.

With rain threatening, the hostess of the picnic called for an immediate end to the volleyball game because the food was ready to be served.

No sooner did Walter give $6,500 to his partner Willie to invest in a liquor store, than Willie disappeared with the money.

Seeing a turtle in the road, Elsa guided it to a safe place in the tall grass.

Shelton's father said again and again, "I wish I had gone to college."

Francis Scott Key, who was on the scene when Fort McHenry was bombarded by a British fleet in 1814, wrote "The Star-Spangled Banner" the very next day.

Pamela bought her house for a very low price because so many other houses in her community were also for sale at the time.

QUESTIONS

1. Who was humane to an animal? _____

2. Who was defrauded? _____

3. Who rued something? _____

4. Who benefited from a glut? _____

5. Who condensed something? _____

6. Who lacked prudence? _____

7. Who was entreated? _____

8. Who was tractable? _____

9. Who was banned? _____

10. Who was subjected to a din? _____

 CONCISE WRITING: Make the following composition more concise. The first paragraph has been rewritten as a sample. Rewrite the other paragraphs, trying to use no more than the number of words suggested.

Some Advice to Employees Who Have Just Joined the Company

Have confidence in those who are supervising your work, as well as in those of the same standing and ability as yourself. They are full of sympathy and consideration for others. If you consult them when you are in need of assistance with something or other, you will find them ready to do a favor for you.   (*Cut to about 25 words, as in the lines below.*)

Have confidence in your supervisors and peers. They are humane. If you consult them when you need help, you will find them obliging.

If a door is closed, knock on that door before you walk in. At no time should you thrust yourself in without receiving a prior invitation to enter.   (*Cut to about 10 words.*)

_____

_____

If you get a job to do that is capable of being done but difficult to do, do not throw up your hands in surrender. Go on with it, in spite of the difficulty.   (*Cut to about 11 words*)

_____

_____

If the person who has employed you ever expresses mild disapproval of you for paying little or no attention to your work, do not take offense but try to do better.   (*Cut to about 17 words.*)

_____

_____

At all times, be open and honest in what you say or do.   (*Cut to 3 words.*)

_____

_____

 CLOSE READING: Read the following statements. Then answer questions 11–20.

STATEMENTS

Mom's message read: "We're safe. Tell you the rest later."

The Boston Tea Party was planned by Samuel Adams with the intention of provoking a war between England and the Thirteen Colonies.

Finding a beautiful, huge, wooden horse outside their walls, the Trojans hauled it into their city. That night, armed Greek warriors emerged from the horse and set fire to Troy.

When John Alden delivered Miles Standish's proposal of marriage to Priscilla, she said, "Why don't you speak for yourself, John?"

When True Son ran away, Cuyloga, his adoptive father, tracked him to his hiding place in the hollow of a tree.

Hearing that a band of Native Americans was approaching his settlement, Tonseten hid himself under his bed.

The Pied Piper played so enchantingly that all the children of Hamelin followed him.

In the middle of the night of April 18, 1775, John Hancock was warned by Paul Revere that British troops were coming to arrest him.

When Secretary of State Seward concluded the purchase of Alaska from Russia in 1867, many Americans called it "Seward's Folly."

Despite military setbacks and shortages of troops and supplies, George Washington refused to give up the fight for independence.

QUESTIONS

11. Who was timid? _____

12. Who led a horde? _____

13. Who was roused? _____

14. Who concocted a conflict? _____

15. Who persisted? _____

16. Who was mocked? _____

17. Who spurned someone? _____

18. Who conveyed the gist of something? _____

19. Who were victims of a sham? _____

20. Who was proficient as a sleuth? _____

 BRAINTEASERS: Fill in the missing letters, as in 1 and 2, below.

---

1. When the grass is **spar** <u>s</u> <u>e</u>, there is little for rabbits to nibble on.

2. Queues   often   form   outside   diners   that   serve **d e l e c** table meals.

3. Shouldn't a store give its **pat** _ _ _ _ s preferred treatment?

4. She said: "Hey, idiot, what time is it?" Wasn't she _ _ **sole** _ _?

5. Consumers are _ **oath** to pay unreasonably high prices.

6. Because of the fog, the ferry was late in getting to its **pie** _.

7. Fighting continues; the _ _ **mist** _ _ _ is being ignored.

8. Hardly anyone laughed; the comedian's jokes were all _ _ **it** _.

9. Was your midnight dip in the ocean just a(n) _ **him**, or did you plan it?

10. Walking uphill is hard, but once past the _ **rest**, the going is easier.

11. She withheld some information from us; she wasn't entirely _ **rank**.

12. Crops that are not picked **with** _ _ in the fields.

13. Jane would like to be a reporter; she has a(n) _ _ **air** for writing.

14. You look **dish** _ _ _ _ _ _; why don't you comb your hair?

15. There are spots in the grass that **tee** _ with ants.

16. You cannot pay bills with **count** _ _ _ _ _ _ money.

17. On December 31, we will be on the **thresh** _ _ _ of a new year.

18. Though the berries look delicious, they are not **comes** _ _ _ _ _.

19. Adventures into the unknown are _ _ **aught** with peril.

20. The winds made it difficult for the firefighters to _ _ **ell** the flames.

LESSON 6

A | **LESSON WORDS 1–10:** Pronounce the word, spell it, study its meanings, and finish the sentence that follows it.

abet (*v.*) encourage with aid or approval; **incite**; **instigate**;
ə-'bet **countenance**

1. It is a (disservice, service) __disservice__ to society to *abet* criminals.

astute (*adj.*) **shrewd**; **clever**; **sagacious**; **crafty**
ə-'st(y)üt

2. One must not be (on, off) __off__ guard with an *astute* opponent.

complex (*adj.*) consisting of interconnected parts; difficult to understand; **complicated**; **intricate**
käm-'pleks

3. A (tablespoon, calculator) __Calculator__ is a *complex* gadget.

conjecture (*n.*) conclusion based on insufficient evidence; **guesswork**; **supposition**
kən-'jek-chər

4. *Conjectures* (sometimes, never) __Sometimes__ turn out to be right.

deter (*v.*) restrain from acting; **discourage**; **dissuade**; **inhibit**
di-'tər

5. Winding roads *deter* (reckless, careful) __Careful__ drivers from increasing their speed.

elude (*v.*) slip away from; **escape**; **evade**; **avoid**
ē-'lüd

6. The convict *eluded* guards and remains (at large, behind bars) __at large__.

eon or **aeon** (*n.*) extremely long and indefinite period of time;
'ē-ən   **age**; **eternity**

7. Our (planet, nation) _planet_ has been in existence for *eons*.

exonerate (*v.*) free from blame or responsibility; **absolve**; **exculpate**; **vindicate**
ig-'zän-ə-ˌrāt

8. Three were found (innocent, ~~guilty~~) _guilty_, and one was *exonerated*.

expedient (*adj.*) suitable under the circumstances; **advantageous**; **advisable**
ik-'spēd-ē-ənt

9. In bad times, a company may find it *expedient* to (increase, reduce) _increase_ its work force.

expire (*v.*) come to an end; **cease**; **terminate**; **die**
ik-'spī(ə)r

10. Licenses *expiring* May 31 should be renewed (on, before) _before_ June 1.

SENTENCE COMPLETION 1–10: Enter the required lesson words.

---

1. The earth's last dinosaurs _expire_**d** many ~~eon~~**eon**s ago.

2. Inez thought it would not be _expedient_ to bring up a(n) _astute_ issue when the members were tired and getting ready to adjourn.

3. Some fear the new policy may _abet_ drug users, rather than _deter_ them.

4. By ___Complex___ twists and turns, the fleet-footed quarter-

back ___eluded___**d** his pursuers.

5. If the charges rest solely on ___Conjecture___, the de-

fendant should be ___exonerate___**d**.

<table>
<tr><td rowspan="2">C</td><td>**SYNONYM ROUNDUP 1–10:** Each completed line should</td></tr>
<tr><td>have three synonyms. Enter the missing letters.</td></tr>
</table>

---

1. abs __ lve	exc __ lp __ te	ex __ n __ rate
2. advantag __ __ us	exped __ __ nt	advis __ ble
3. __ __ cape	el __ de	ev __ de
4. comp __ __ cated	__ __ __ plex	intr __ c __ te
5. cl __ v __ r	ast __ te	shr __ w __
6. c __ __ se	d __ __	__ __ pire
7. e __ n	__ ge	__ ternity
8. disc __ __ rage	dis __ __ ade	d __ t __ r
9. g __ __ sswork	s __ pposition	__ __ __ jecture
10. __ __ cite	ab __ t	c __ __ ntenance

<table>
<tr><td rowspan="2">D</td><td>**LESSON WORDS 11–20:** Pronounce the word, spell it, study</td></tr>
<tr><td>its meanings, and finish the sentence that follows it.</td></tr>
</table>

---

inclement (*adj.*) **stormy; rough; harsh; severe**
in-'klem-ənt

11. *Inclement* weather keeps most people (outdoors,

indoors) ___indoors___.

iota (*n.*)   very small quantity; infinitesimal amount; **bit; jot; mite;**
ī-'ōt-ə   **smidgen**

> 12. There is not an *iota* of doubt that the earth is (round, flat)
> _round_____.

jibe (*v.*)   be in accord; **agree; correspond; conform**
'jīb

> 13. Fans (boo, approve) _boo_____ when an umpire's de-
> cision does not *jibe* with their expectations.

lethal (*adj.*)   causing or capable of causing death; **deadly; fatal;**
'lē-thəl   **mortal**

> 14. We must be aware that carbon (monoxide, dioxide)
> _monoxide_____ is a *lethal* gas.

maim (*v.*)   wound seriously; **cripple; mutilate; disfigure**
'mām

> 15. The pirate with the wooden (club, leg) _leg_____ had
> been *maimed* in battle.

mediocre (*adj.*)   neither good nor bad; barely adequate; **average;**
ˌmēd-ē-'ō-kər   **inferior**

> 16. Food prices (rise, fall) _rise_____ whenever crops are
> *mediocre.*

obsolete (*adj.*)   no longer in use; **old-fashioned; outmoded;**
ˌäb-sə-'lēt   **out-of-date**

> 17. Rail travel made the (stagecoach, automobile)
> _stagecoach_____ *obsolete.*

thrive (*v.*)   be fortunate; be successful; **prosper; flourish**
'thrīv

> 18. Those who (shun, seek) _shun_____ work are not likely
> to *thrive.*

trek (*n.*)   **journey; expedition; trip**
'trek

> 19. (Planes, Books) _Books_____ take us on *treks* to dis-
> tant times and places.

wane (*v.*) decrease in power, size, or extent; **abate**; **ebb**; **sub-**
'wān   **side**

> 20. As daylight *wanes*, the streetlights are gradually turned
>
> (on, off) _~~on~~_ .

SENTENCE COMPLETION 11–20: Enter the required lesson words from D, above.

---

1. Department-store sales were _mediocre_ this past
   week because of the _inclement_ weather.

2. If fireworks are inexpertly used or are defective, they can
   maim people, or even be _lethal_ .

3. Your story _jibe_ s perfectly with his; there is not a(n)
   ~~wane~~ iota of difference between them.

4. In today's fiercely competitive business world, manufacturers
   who use _iota_ equipment cannot possibly
   thrive .

5. We encountered so many difficulties in our last _trek_
   through the woods that my enthusiasm for hiking has
   obsolete d.

SYNONYM ROUNDUP 11–20: Each line, when completed,
should have three words similar in meaning. Fill in the missing letters.

---

11. __ bb   w __ ne   __ bate

12. i __ ta   b __ t   sm __ dg __ n

13. st __ rmy	r __ __ gh	incl __ m __ nt
14. tr __ p	tr __ k	exp __ d __ tion
15. thr __ ve	pr __ sp __ r	fl __ __ rish
16. __ aim	__ ripple	m __ t __ late
17. __ gree	j __ be	cor __ __ spond
18. av __ r __ ge	inf __ r __ __ r	medioc __ __
19. d __ __ dly	leth __ __	f __ t __ l
20. outm __ ded	old-fash __ __ ned	__ __ solete

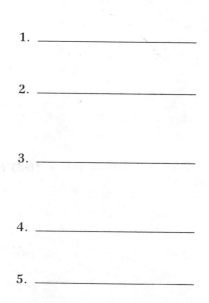

SYNONYMS: To avoid repetition, replace the boldfaced word with a synonym from the vocabulary list below.

**complicated   evade   expedition   inferior   inhibit
instigate   outmoded   prosper   sagacious   terminate**

1. We want excellence, not mediocrity; we will not be satisfied
with **mediocre** results.

1. _____

2. Yours is a **complex** problem;
mine is of much lesser complex-
ity.

2. _____

3. That was a very **astute** move
on your part; we are truly
amazed by your remarkable astuteness.

3. _____

4. New equipment begins to obso-
lesce the day it is manufac-
tured; in a few years it may well
be **obsolete**.

4. _____

5. Bad weather is usually a deter-
rent, but it did not **deter** us
from finishing our game.

5. _____

6. Our policy is about to **expire**; the expiration data is imminent.

6. _____

7. The suspect is elusive; he has again **eluded** his pursuers.

7. _____**d**

8. They trekked through unexplored forest; it was a perilous **trek**.

8. _____

9. Your competitors do a thriving business. Why don't you **thrive**?

9. _____

10. We certainly did not **abet** the protestors; someone else must have been the abettor.

10. _____

ANTONYMS: Enter the word most nearly the antonym of the boldfaced word or words. Choose your antonyms from the following list.

absolve	advisable	deadly	dissuade	supposition
expire	incite	intricate	smidgen	subside

1. What I thought was a **simple** problem turned out to be quite

   _____.

2. People and animals need food to **live**; without it, they

   would _____.

3. If the pain **increases**, I take my medicine and it begins to

   _____.

4. In crisis situations, actions normally **inexpedient** may be

   very definitely _____.

5. He **did not abet** the rioters; someone else

   _____**d** them.

6. The testimony may _____ the suspect, rather than **incriminate** her.

7. There was not a **large amount** of leftovers—just a(n)

   _____.

8. Is this a **conclusion based on sufficient evidence**, or a(n)

  _____?

9. I didn't **encourage** her to resign; in fact, I tried to

  _____ her.

10. Smoking is decidely not a **harmless** habit; it can be

  _____.

 CONCISE WRITING: Express the thought of each sentence in NO MORE THAN FOUR WORDS.

---

1. Rocks endure for extremely long and indefinite periods of time.

  _____

2. The grades that Lori has been getting are neither good nor bad.

  _____

3. Some accidents cause people to lose an arm, a leg, or the sight of an eye.

  _____

4. The conclusions that you have arrived at are in accord with mine.

  _____

5. Take whatever course of action is suitable under the circumstances.

  _____

6. The person who had been on trial was freed of all blame.

  _____

ANALOGIES: Which lettered pair of words—**a, b, c, d,** or **e**—most nearly has the same relationship as the numbered pair? Enter the letter of your answer in the space provided.

1. FLOURISH : SUCCESSFUL

    a. scoff : respectful   *b.* work : unemployed
    c. persevere : persistent   *d.* cower : unafraid
    e. prevail : inferior   1. _____

2. OBSOLETE : CURRENT

    a. loath : willing   *b.* abundant : plentiful
    c. adept : proficient   *d.* humane : altruistic
    e. uncivil : insolent   2. _____

3. MEDIOCRE : DISTINCTION

    a. invaluable : worth   *b.* insignificant : importance
    c. doubtful : uncertainty   *d.* outstanding : merit
    e. complicated : difficulty   3. _____

4. CULPABLE : EXONERATE

    a. needy : assist   *b.* lost : direct
    c. sincere : believe   *d.* obliging : thank
    e. mistaken : heed   4. _____

5. COMPLEX : GRASP

    a. rare : find   *b.* brittle : break
    c. luscious : consume   *d.* obvious : perceive
    e. painless : endure   5. _____

6. LETHAL : FATALITY

    a. perfect : flaw   *b.* fragile : hardness
    c. vague : misunderstanding *d.* simple : mystery
    e. perishable : freshness   6. _____

7. WANE : IMPORTANCE

    a. mature : age   *b.* recuperate : health
    c. prosper : wealth   *d.* shrink : size
    e. fail : disappointment   7. _____

LESSON 7

 LESSON WORDS 1–10: Pronounce the word, spell it, study its meanings, and finish the sentence that follows it.

---

adamant (*adj.*) unyielding in attitude or opinion; **inflexible**;
ˈad-ə-mənt   **uncompromising**

1. Mediators may give (in, up) _____ if the opposing sides remain *adamant*.

boost (*v.*) lift by pushing up from below; **raise**; **increase**;
ˈbüst   **augment**

2. The (jeers, cheers) _____ from the stands *boosted* our team's morale.

concede (*v.*) admit grudgingly; **acknowledge**; **grant**
kən-ˈsēd

3. The losers *conceded* that (we, they) _____ were the better team.

device (*n.*) something devised or constructed for a particular pur-
di-ˈvīs   pose; **invention**; **contrivance**; **gadget**

4. A (zipper, spool) _____ is a *device* for joining two pieces of cloth.

estimate (*v.*) calculate approximately; **judge**; **figure**; **reckon**
ˈes-tə-ˌmāt

5. If you ask me to *estimate* a distance, I will tell you (roughly, exactly) _____ what I think it is.

extraction (*n.*) **origin**; **birth**; **ancestry**; **descent**; **lineage**
ik-ˈstrak-shən

6. The ancestors of (most, all) _____ of us Americans, except Native Americans, were of foreign *extraction*.

foreboding (*n.*) strong inner conviction of a coming misfortune;
(')fór-'bōd-iŋ **apprehension; premonition; misgiving**

  7. We had a *foreboding* that we would (win, lose) _____ .

immaterial (*adj.*) of no essential consequence; **unimportant**;
'im-ə-'tir-ē-əl **irrelevant**

  8. The fact that I had forgotten my key was *immaterial* because my folks were home (before, after) _____ me.

impetus (*n.*) driving force; **impulse; stimulus**
'im-pət-əs

  9. The possibility of a salary (freeze, increase) _____ is an *impetus* to a greater effort.

induce (*v.*) move someone to do something; **influence; persuade**
in-'d(y)üs **suade**

  10. Logic cannot *induce* (reasonable, enraged) _____ people to change their minds.

SENTENCE COMPLETION 1–10: Enter the required lesson words.

---

1. Many Americans who are not of Irish _____ enjoy wearing green on St. Patrick's Day; the fact that they are not Irish is _____ .

2. On March 15, 44 B.C., Julius Caesar's wife had a(n) _____ of evil and begged her husband to stay home, but she could not _____ him to obey her.

3. Even the most _____ foes of the proposed legisla-

   tion _____ that they cannot stop it from becoming

   a law.

4. A jet engine is the _____ that produces an airliner's

   forward _____.

5. The corporation's president confidentially _____s

   that its new product could _____ earnings ten per-

   cent in the coming year.

C **SYNONYM ROUNDUP 1–10:** Each completed line should have three synonyms. Enter the missing letters.

---

1. con __ __ de   gr __ nt   a __ knowl __ __ ge

2. contriv __ nce   __ __ vice   g __ dg __ t

3. inflex __ ble   __ __ compromising   ad __ m __ nt

4. j __ dge   est __ m __ te   r __ ck __ n

5. __ __ __ giving   __ __ __ __ boding   appre __ __ __ sion

6. or __ g __ n   des __ ent   __ __ traction

7. p __ rs __ ade   __ __ fluence   indu __ __

8. r __ __ se   incr __ __ se   boo __ __

9. stim __ l __ s   __ __ petus   __ __ pulse

10. __ __ important   __ __ relevant   __ __ material

LESSON WORDS 11–20: Pronounce the word, spell it, study its meanings, and finish the sentence that follows it.

---

legendary (*adj.*)   fabled in legend or tradition; **well-known**; **fa-**
'lej-ən-ˌder-ē   **mous**; **fabulous**

   11. It is extremely (easy, hard) _____ to get tickets to the *legendary* violinist's rare concerts.

notorious (*adj.*)   widely but unfavorably known; **infamous**; **ill-**
nō-'tȯr-ē-əs   **famed**

   12. (Many, Few) _____ were aware of the *notorious* dealer's reputation.

obstruct (*v.*)   block or close off by obstacles; **impede**; **hinder**;
äb-'strəkt   **bar**

   13. A(n) (overturned, speeding) _____ ve-hicle was *obstructing* traffic.

opportune (*adj.*)   especially right or suitable; **timely**; **favorable**;
ˌäp-ər-'t(y)ün   **propitious**

   14. Rain came at an *opportune* time; the reservoirs were (dry, full) _____ .

plummet (*v.*)   drop or fall sharply and abruptly; **plunge**;
'pləm-ət   **nosedive**

   15. A sudden (glut, dearth) _____ of tomatoes causes the price per pound to *plummet*.

repulse (*v.*)   drive back; beat back; **repel**; **check**
ri-'pəls

   16. When our foes are *repulsed*, (they, we) _____ suffer a setback.

stamina (*n.*)   physical or moral strength to withstand hardship;
'stam-ə-nə   **endurance**; **perseverance**

   17. (Brawny, Frail) _____ people seem to lack *stamina* for heavy work.

subjugate (*v.*) bring under complete control; **conquer**; **subdue**;
ˈsəb-ji-ˌgāt **crush**; **vanquish**

18. A *subjugated* nation (loses, gains) ＿＿＿＿＿＿＿＿ its independence.

unwavering (*adj.*) not fluctuating or hesitant; **firm**; **sure**;
ˌən-ˈwāv-(ə-)riŋ **steady**; **unfaltering**

19. Their support is *unwavering*; they (usually, always)
＿＿＿＿＿＿＿＿＿＿ back us.

venture (*n.*) risky or dangerous undertaking; **adventure**; **enter-**
ˈven-chər **prise**

20. Business *ventures* are not for people who are (loath, inclined) ＿＿＿＿＿＿＿＿＿ to take chances.

SENTENCE COMPLETION 11–20: Enter the required lesson words from D, above.

---

1. The outnumbered defenders feared that their country would be

   ruthlessly ＿＿＿＿＿＿＿＿＿**d** if they could not de-

   cisively ＿＿＿＿＿＿＿＿ the invaders at the mountain pass.

2. Prices were ＿＿＿＿＿＿＿＿**ing**; it was a(n) exceptionally

   ＿＿＿＿＿＿＿＿＿ time to buy.

3. The ＿＿＿＿＿＿＿＿ criminal's only hope of avoiding con-

   viction was to try to ＿＿＿＿＿＿＿＿＿ justice by bribing one

   of the jurors.

4. We were stunned when the favorite, who is _____

   for her _____, failed to complete the first lap in

   the 1600-meter race.

5. In their _____ to win independence, the leaders of

   the American Revolution lacked the _____

   support of the majority of Americans.

SYNONYM ROUNDUP 11–20: Each line, when completed, should have three words similar in meaning. Fill in the missing letters.

---

11. endur __ nce	st __ m __ na	p __ rs __ v __ rance
12. fam __ __ s	l __ g __ nd __ ry	well-kn __ __ n
13. __ __ famous	n __ t __ rious	ill-f __ m __ d
14. obstr __ ct	h __ nd __ r	__ __ pede
15. pl __ nge	n __ sed __ ve	plum __ __ t
16. r __ p __ l	ch __ ck	__ __ pulse
17. st __ __ dy	unf __ ltering	__ __ wavering
18. subd __ __	vanq __ __ sh	__ __ __ jugate
19. t __ m __ ly	opp __ rt __ ne	prop __ t __ ous
20. v __ nt __ re	__ __ terprise	ad __ __ __ __ ture

SYNONYMS: To avoid repetition, replace the boldfaced word or expression with a synonym from the vocabulary list.

persuade	gadget	subdue	inflexible	reckon
fabulous	propitious	descent	infamous	impede

1. The athlete most responsible for the fame of the New York Yankees was Babe Ruth, their **famous** home-run hitter.

1. _____

2. Sue **estimated** that we would have a capacity crowd on opening night, and her estimate proved to be correct.

2. _____**ed**

3. A fallen tree trunk **obstructed** our advance, but we were able to climb over that obstruction.

3. _____**d**

4. The emperor Napoleon conquered most of Europe, but he could not **conquer** Russia.

4. _____

5. Our classmate Maria is of Hispanic **ancestry**; her ancestors lived in Puerto Rico.

5. _____

6. As a further inducement, the store lowered prices an additional 10%, but that **induced** only a few more customers to make purchases.

6. _____**d**

7. It is not yet fully known how the authorities were able to bring the **widely but unfavorably known** financier to justice.

7. _____

8. Your **uncompromising** attitude makes compromise impossible.

8. _____

9. The weather has turned inclement; it is certainly not a
timely time for a stroll.   9. _____

10. Inventors have devised a va-
riety of **devices** for simpli-
fying household tasks.   10. _____ **s**

**endurance   legendary   hinder   augment   acknowledge
irrelevant   subjugate   favorable   plunge   unfaltering**

1. The hawk _____ **d** earthward, seized its
prey, and **soared**.

2. The American-led invasion of Europe in 1944 **liberated** nation
after   nation   that   the   Nazis   and   their   allies   had

_____ **d**.

3. They _____ **ed** your progress; we did **not
bar** your way.

4. An increase in food prices is _____
when one is very wealthy, but **of vital consequence** when
one is very poor.

5. They _____ **d** that we outplayed them in
the last two games, but they still **do not concede** that ours is
the better team.

6. The sales staff was _____ **ed** for the holi-
day shopping season and **reduced** as soon as it was over.

7. I expect my **weakness** to subside and my _____
to return.

8. It was an **inopportune** time for her to ask for a raise; she

should have chosen a more _____ occasion.

9. By his achievements in the 1936 Olympics, Jesse Owens, a prac-
tically **unknown** athlete, became a(n) _____
hero.

10. Despite **wavering** support from some of the voters, the candidate was _____ in her determination to
go on with her campaign.

 CONCISE WRITING: Express the thought of each sentence
in NO MORE THAN FOUR WORDS.

---

1. Pizarro brought the people who were living in Peru under his
complete control.

_____

2. Once in a while, everyone of us has strong inner convictions of
approaching misfortune.

_____

3. Those who took part in the invasion were driven back.

_____

4. Did the risky undertaking that she entered into turn out to be a
success?

_____

5. The questions that they asked were of no essential consequence.

_____

6. Some people do not have the physical or moral strength to withstand hardship.

_____

ANALOGIES: Which lettered pair of words—**a, b, c, d,** or **e**— most nearly has the same relationship as the numbered pair? Enter the letter of your answer in the space provided.

1. INVINCIBLE : SUBJUGATE

   a. truthful : believe   *b.* corruptible : bribe
   c. adamant : persuade   *d.* flexible : influence
   e. employable : hire   1. _____

2. INFAMOUS : NOTORIOUS

   a. costly : inexpensive   *b.* intricate : simple
   c. obsolete : new   *d.* trite : stale
   e. harmless : lethal   2. _____

3. MISGIVING : ANXIETY

   a. tornado : destruction   *b.* setback : rejoicing
   c. antiseptic : infection   *d.* paint : wood
   e. reassurance : uncertainty   3. _____

4. WEATHER VANE : DEVICE

   a. plastic : metal   *b.* hut : dwelling
   c. seed : plant   *d.* acquaintance : relative
   e. lining : garment   4. _____

5. TEST PILOT : VENTURESOME

   a. job application : unkempt   *b.* pupil : inattentive
   c. sophomore : illiterate   *d.* beneficiary : ungrateful
   e. goalie : vigilant   5. _____

6. UNCOMPROMISING : FLEXIBILITY

   a. crafty : astuteness   *b.* mediocre : excellence
   c. biased : prejudice   *d.* imperfect : shortcoming
   e. civil : manners   6. _____

7. IMPETUS : MOVE

   a. fog : see   *b.* lullaby : sleep
   c. din : relax   *d.* gag : speak
   e. illness : work   7. _____

LESSON 8

 LESSON WORDS 1–10: Pronounce the word, spell it, study its meanings, and finish the sentence that follows it.

affluent (*adj.*) having abundant goods or riches; **wealthy; pros-**
'af-(ˌ)lü-ənt   **perous; opulent**

1. You don't have to be *affluent* to own a (calculator, yacht)
_____ .

aloof (*adj.*) distant in feeling or interest; **unconcerned; indif-**
ə-'lüf   **ferent**

2. (Selfish, Humane) _____ people remain *aloof* when others suffer.

bolster (*v.*) prop up; **support; sustain**
'bōl-stər

3. The (ominous, propitious) _____ news *bolstered* our spirits.

chore (*n.*) small routine job around a house or farm; **task; as-**
'chȯ(ə)r   **signment**

4. My *chore* this week is to (expand, vacuum) _____ the living room.

commitment (*n.*) agreement to do something in the future;
kə-'mit-mənt   **pledge; promise**

5. If you say you (may, will) _____ come, you are making a *commitment*.

confederate (*n.*) person allied with another or others; **accom-**
kən-'fed-(ə-)rət   **plice; ally**

6. The bank robber was (arrested, aided) _____ by a *confederate*.

63

convert (*v.*) change in form from one state to another; **trans-**
kən-'vərt   **form; alter**

     7. (Falling, rising) _____ temperatures *convert*
        slush to ice.

covet (*v.*) wish for enviously or excessively; **desire; crave**
'kəv-ət

     8. (Jealous, Generous) _____ youngsters *covet*
        their playmates' toys.

crestfallen (*adj.*) with hanging head; **dejected; disheartened;**
'krest-ˌfȯ-lən   **downcast**

     9. The (vanquished, victorious) _____
        contender was *crestfallen*.

infer (*v.*) reach a conclusion by reasoning from facts; **conclude;**
in-'fər   **deduce**

     10. If the lights are (out, on) _____ , we may *infer* the store
        is closed.

 SENTENCE COMPLETION 1–10: Enter the required lesson
words.

---

1. While Cinderella swept ashes from the hearth and did all the

   other unpleasant _____**s**, her smiling stepsisters

   stood _____ .

2. By _____**ing** the spirits of the _____

   players, the coach got them to rally and to win the game.

3. Though the actress's successful movies have made her

   _____ , they have not won her what she

   _____**s** most—an Oscar.

4. Lady Macbeth, by goading her husband, _____**s**

   his loyalty to King Duncan into a(n) _____

   to murder him.

5. The evidence led investigators to _____ that the pris-

   oner could not have escaped without help from a(n)

   _____ .

SYNONYM ROUNDUP 1–10: Each completed line should have three synonyms. Enter the missing letters.

---

1. accompli __ e   all __   conf __ d __ r __ te
2. al __ __ f   __ __ concerned   __ __ different
3. ch __ nge   alt __ r   __ __ __ vert
4. concl __ de   __ __ fer   ded __ ce
5. des __ re   __ rave   c __ v __ t
6. __ __ __ heartened   __ __ jected   crestfall __ __
7. prom __ se   ple __ ge   __ __ __ mitment
8. pr __ sp __ rous   affl __ ent   op __ lent
9. b __ lst __ r   s __ pport   sust __ __ n
10. t __ sk   assi __ nment   __ __ ore

LESSON WORDS 11–20: Pronounce the word, spell it, study its meanings, and finish the sentence that follows it.

---

mar (*v.*) detract from the perfectness of; **spoil**; **damage**; **im-**
ˈmär   **pair**; **tarnish**

   11. We won, but an (injury, award) _____ to a
       player *marred* our victory.

obliterate (*v.*)   remove all traces of; destroy utterly; **erase; efface**
ə-'blit-ə-,rāt

    12. Use a(n) (comma, eraser) _____ to *obliterate*
         what you have written.

rile (*v.*)   make angry or resentful; **irritate; provoke; peeve**
'rī(ə)l

    13. A close decision against our (team, foes) _____
         riles us.

robust (*adj.*)   strong and healthy; **hardy; vigorous**
rō-'bəst

    14. After a(n) (vacation, illness) _____ , one is un-
         likely to look *robust*.

site (*n.*)   place where something is or was; **location; point; spot**
'sīt

    15. We   looked   for   Franklin's   (birthplace,   writings)
         _____ , but we couldn't find the *site*.

steep (*adj.*)   sharply rising or falling; **abrupt; precipitous; sheer**
'stēp

    16. A vehicle gains speed as it goes (up, down) _____ a
         steep slope.

surface (*n.*)   outermost or uppermost layer or area; **top; exte-**
'sər-fəs   **rior; outside**

    17. At night, (all, half) _____ the earth's *surface* is
         cloaked in darkness.

thwart (*v.*)   prevent (someone) from achieving a purpose; **frus-**
'thwȯ(ə)rt   **trate; foil; baffle**

    18. Loafers are *thwarted* when they cannot (find, avoid)
         _____ work.

turbulence (*n.*)   state of wild disorder; **commotion; agitation;**
'tər-byə-lən(t)s   **turmoil**

    19. On a (calm, windy) _____ day, there is no *turbu-*
         lence in the atmosphere.

vestige (*n.*)   visible mark left by something vanished; **relic**; **trace**
ˈves-tij

    20. (Soaring, Plummeting) _____ tempera-
        tures removed all *vestiges* of yesterday's snow.

SENTENCE COMPLETION 11–20: Enter the required lesson words from D, above.

1. If you were repeatedly _____**ed** in your at-

   tempts to talk to the manager by being put on hold, wouldn't you

   be _____**d**?

2. A couple of objects, probably snowballs, struck our windshield

   but did not _____ its _____ .

3. The _____**er** the hill, the more _____ a jog-

   ger has to be to make it unwinded to the top.

4. Boats carefully avoid the waters close to the falls because of the

   river's _____ at that _____.

5. The devastating eruption of Vesuvius that occurred in A.D. 79

   _____**d** Pompeii from the face of the earth,

   leaving no _____ of that flourishing Italian town.

SYNONYM ROUNDUP 11–20: Each line, when completed,
should have three words similar in meaning. Fill in the missing letters.

11. t __ rmoil   __ __ __ motion   t __ rb __ lence

12. abr __ pt   st __ __ p   prec __ p __ tous

13. b __ ffle   fr __ str __ te   __ __ wart

14. t __ rn __ sh   sp __ __ l   m __ r

15. __ bl __ terate   __ rase   __ __ face

16. hard __   v __ g __ rous   r __ b __ st

17. irr __ tate   p __ __ ve   __ ile

18. l __ c __ tion   sp __ t   sit __

19. s __ rf __ ce   t __ p   __ __ terior

20. r __ lic   tr __ ce   v __ st __ ge

G   **SYNONYMS:** replace the boldfaced word or expression with
     a synonym from the word list below:

---

indifferent	pledge	relic	sustain	tarnish
opulent	provoke	hardy	chore	dejected

1. Some are **disheartened** when
   they lose a game, but others do
   not take such matters to heart.   1. _____

2. When I finish this task, I have
   other little **tasks** to do.   2. _____**s**

3. As we retraced our steps, we
   saw **traces** that we had not noticed previously of an oil slick
   that had washed ashore.   3. _____**s**

4. If you become **rich**, what will
   you do with your riches?   4. _____

5. Our allies needed support; if we
   had not **supported** them, they
   might have collapsed.   5. _____**ed**

6. A spoilsport may say or do things to **spoil** a happy occasion.

6. _____

7. She was angry at me, though I had done nothing to **make** her **angry**.

7. _____

8. Some showed concern for the victim; others seemed **unconcerned**.

8. _____

9. Though the contestants all look **vigorous**, some may not have the vigor to finish the marathon.

9. _____

10. He promised to join, but he didn't keep his **promise**.

10. _____

ANTONYMS: In the blank in each sentence below, enter the word most nearly the antonym of the boldfaced word or words. Choose your antonyms from the following list.

---

exterior	frustrate	transform	downcast	precipitous
spurn	prosperous	aloof	bolster	turmoil

1. Many who used to **crave** cigarettes now _____ them when offered.

2. All of us are **overjoyed** at the good news, but why are you _____?

3. Through hard work, Andrew Carnegie, a very **poor** immigrant, became one of the most _____ Americans of his time.

4. What goes on **inside** the earth is not usually visible on its _____ .

5. While one group was trying to _____ the struggling new government, others were doing their best to **pull out the props from under** it.

6. We enjoy the **calm** that follows the _____ of a storm.

7. Sometimes circumstances **help** us achieve our purpose, and at other times they _____ us.

8. The entrance was completely _____**ed**; the rest of the house was **not altered**.

9. We cannot remain _____ when there is damage to the environment; we must be deeply **concerned**.

10. **Gradual** price increases are a nuisance, but _____ ones are altogether intolerable.

 CONCISE WRITING: Express the thought of each sentence in NO MORE THAN FOUR WORDS

---

1. People in foreign lands enviously wish for the freedoms that we enjoy.

    _____

2. No one made any agreements to do anything in the future.

    _____

3. What was the conclusion that you arrived at by the process of reasoning?

    _____

4. Showers detracted from the perfectness of the parade that we took part in.

    _____

5. Patricia finished the small routine jobs that she has to do.

    _____

6. The person that he is allied with is widely but unfavorably known.

    _____

J   **ANALOGIES:** Which lettered pair of words—**a, b, c, d,** or **e**—most nearly has the same relationship as the numbered pair? Enter the letter of your answer in the space provided.

1. OPULENT : INCOME

   a. mediocre : talent   *b.* reckless : caution
   c. popular : following   *d.* astute : trap
   e. clumsy : skill   1. _____

2. INDIFFERENT : CONCERN

   a. culpable : blame   *b.* untidy : neatness
   c. antagonistic : hostility *d.* rueful : regret
   e. obliging : favors   2. _____

3. CONVERT : TRANSFORMATION

   a. obstruct : access   *b.* repair : defect
   c. pledge : commitment   *d.* concede : denial
   e. repay : debt   3. _____

4. IRRITABLE : RILE

   a. unruly : control   *b.* adamant : persuade
   c. determined : thwart   *d.* prudent : outwit
   e. unwary : bilk   4. _____

5. MARRED : SPOILED

   a. banned : interdicted   *b.* relished : disliked
   c. unchanged : converted   *d.* encouraged : deterred
   e. soared : plummeted   5. _____

6. PRECIPITOUS : ASCEND

   a. comestible : eat   *b.* legible : read
   c. uncomplicated : grasp   *d.* intolerable : bear
   e. inconspicuous : overlook   6. _____

7. COVETOUS : ENVY

   a. garrulous : shyness   *b.* timid : misgiving
   c. despairing : hope   *d.* dishonest : candor
   e. penniless : affluence   7. _____

LESSON 9

 LESSON WORDS 1–10: Pronounce the word, spell it, study its meanings, and finish the sentence that follows it.

---

adage (*n.*)   old saying commonly accepted as a truth; **proverb**;
'ad-ij   **byword**

    1. The *adage* "Haste makes waste" cautions us not to (delay, hurry) _____ .

cajole (*v.*)   persuade by flattery or promises; **coax**; **wheedle**;
kə-'jōl   **sweet-talk**

    2. People who (like, hate) _____ to be overpraised cannot be *cajoled.*

chagrin (*n.*)   mental distress caused by failure or disappointment;
shə-'grin   **shame; mortification; humiliation**

    3. To their *chagrin*, the world champions finished (last, first) _____ .

clique (*n.*)   narrow, small, exclusive group of people; **circle**;
'klēk   **coterie; set**

    4. The members of a *clique* usually (welcome, reject) _____ outsiders.

derogatory (*adj.*)   expressing a low opinion; **belittling; dispar-**
di-'räg-ə-ˌtór-ē   **aging; slighting**

    5. It is *derogatory* to be called a (whiz, dolt) _____ .

dispel (*v.*)   drive away; **scatter; dissipate**
dis-'pel

    6. The (setting, rising) _____ sun *dispelled* the fog.

fad (*n.*)   fashion or manner of conduct followed for a time; **style**;
'fad   **craze**; **rage**

>   7. Conservatives tend to (reject, embrace) _____
>   a new *fad*.

illustrious (*adj.*)   highly   distinguished;   **eminent**;   **famous**;
il-'əs-trē-əs   **renowned**

>   8. People are (eager, loath) _____ to see *illustrious*
>   performers.

incarcerate (*v.*)   put in prison; **jail**; **confine**
in-'kär-sə-ˌrāt

>   9. Convicts are *incarcerated* in the state (legislature, peniten-
>   tiary) _____ .

indignation (*n.*)   righteous anger; strong displeasure; **ire**; **wrath**
ˌin-dig-'nā-shən

>   10. (Victims, Scofflaws) _____ deserve the
>   public's *indignation*.

B   **SENTENCE COMPLETION 1–10:** Enter the required lesson
words.

---

1. Elsie's _____ was aroused when she heard
   that Bill, whom she had often helped with his homework, was

   making _____ remarks about her.

2. It was much to the _____ of the zookeeper that,

   with a large crowd looking on, he could not _____
   the lioness back into her cage.

3. Janice felt that she would have to follow the latest

   _____s in attire to be accepted into Marcy's

   _____ .

4. Many _____ prisoners, like Sir Walter

Raleigh and the Earl of Essex, were _____**d**
in the infamous Tower of London.

5. Carl tried to _____ my sadness by reciting the

_____ "It is always darkest just before the dawn."

SYNONYM ROUNDUP 1–10: Each completed line should have three synonyms. Enter the missing letters.

---

1. b __ l __ ttling	disp __ r __ ging	der __ g __ tory
2. c __ nf __ ne	j __ __ l	incar __ erate
3. cl __ que	cir __ le	c __ t __ rie
4. cr __ ze	st __ le	f __ d
5. em __ nent	fam __ __ s	ill __ str __ __ __ s
6. pr __ v __ rb	ad __ ge	__ __ word
7. sc __ tter	d __ sp __ l	dis __ __ pate
8. ch __ gr __ n	sh __ me	h __ mil __ __ tion
9. wh __ __ dle	c __ __ x	c __ j __ le
10. wr __ th	__ re	ind __ __ nation

LESSON WORDS 11–20: Pronounce the word, spell it, study its meanings, and finish the sentence that follows it.

---

linger (*v.*) be slow in leaving; **tarry**; **loiter**; **stay**
ˈliŋ-gər

    11. I might have *lingered* if I had (nothing, chores)

_____ to do.

numb (*adj.*)   deprived of the power to feel or move; **deadened**;
'nəm   **paralyzed**; **desensitized**

> 12. That day, I couldn't (budge, breathe) _____;
>   I was *numb* with fear.

ostentatious (*adj.*)   intended to attract notice; **pretentious**;
ˌäs-tən-'tā-shəs   **showy**; **splashy**

> 13. Coming to school by (bus, limousine) _____
>   may be considered *ostentatious*.

plausible (*adj.*)   apparently worthy of belief; **credible**; **believ-**
'plȯ-zə-bəl   **able**

> 14. There can be (no, some) _____ doubt about the truth
>   of a *plausible* excuse.

probe (*n.*)   searching examination; **investigation**; **inquiry**
'prōb

> 15. A *probe* must not (ignore, investigate) _____
>   rumors.

prodigious (*adj.*)   of great size, power, or extent; **enormous**;
prə-'dij-əs   **huge**; **immense**

> 16. (Chickens, Oxen) _____ are legendary for their
>   *prodigious* strength.

rankle (*v.*)   cause bitter resentment in; **irritate**; **embitter**; **in-**
'raŋ-kəl   **flame**

> 17. When they (evade, keep) _____ their commit-
>   ments, elected officials *rankle* the voters.

scant (*adj.*)   not quite enough; **meager**; **insufficient**
'skant

> 18. The Devils led by a *scant* margin; the score was 31 to
>   (30, 12) _____.

surveillance (*n.*)   close watch; **supervision**; **scrutiny**
sər-'vā-lən(t)s

> 19. *Surveillance* of the ruler's residence was (tightened, re-
>   laxed) _____ after several threats.

sustain (*v.*) bear up under; **endure**; **undergo**; **suffer**
sə-'stān

20. The physician considers the patient too (robust, frail)
_____ to *sustain* surgery.

SENTENCE COMPLETION 11–20: Enter the required lesson words from D, above.

---

1. Throughout the yearlong _____ of the jewelry theft, the chief suspects were continuously under police _____ .

2. The evidence is too _____ to make a(n) _____ case against any of the suspects.

3. The losses that investors _____**ed** in the stock market crash of 1929 were _____ .

4. Marie Antoinette's _____ wardrobe and banquets _____**d** the French common people.

5. We couldn't _____ any longer at the picnic because our hands and feet were turning _____ from the cold.

SYNONYM ROUNDUP 11–20: Each line, when completed, should have three words similar in meaning. Fill in the missing letters.

---

11. bel __ __ vable   cred __ ble   pl __ __ s __ ble

12. d __ __ dened   paral __ zed   n __ __ b

13. enorm __ __ s   prodig __ __ __ s   h __ ge

14. inq __ __ ry   in __ __ stigation   __ __ obe

15. irr __ tate   __ ankle   __ __ bitter

16. __ cant   m __ __ ger   insuffic __ __ nt

17. pretent __ __ __ s   show __   __ __ tentatious

18. s __ ffer   under __ __   sust __ __ n

19. s __ pervis __ __ n   scr __ t __ ny   surv __ __ llance

20. t __ rry   l __ nger   l __ __ ter

Ⓖ **SYNONYMS:** To avoid repetition, replace the boldfaced word or expression with a synonym from the vocabulary below.

---

mortification   **coterie**   **inquiry**   **endure**   **ire**
scrutiny   **eminent**   **wheedle**   **proverb**   **pretentious**

1. At the time they were under **close watch**, they had no idea that they were being watched.

1. _____

2. Why are you indignant? What did I do to arouse your **indignation**?

2. _____

3. One of my neighbors tries to impress others by wearing flashy clothes, but the others are not **flashy** dressers.

3. _____

4. Though they have **suffered** many financial losses, their style of living does not seem to have suffered.

4. _____d

5. An old **saying** says, "Empty barrels make loud noises."

5. _____

6. Imagine my **humiliation**! Never had I felt so humiliated!

6. _____

7. Don't try to **sweet-talk** us; we don't respond to sweet-talk.

7. _____

8. I object to your **small exclusive group** because it excludes outsiders.

8. _____

9. Our **highly distinguished** guest of honor has distinguished herself in many ways.

9. _____

10. A team of skilled investigators is conducting the **investigation**.

10. _____

ANTONYMS: In the space provided in each sentence below, enter the word most nearly the antonym of the boldfaced word or words. Choose your antonyms from the following list.

credible	loiter	meager	slighting	showy
immense	intern	renowned	desensitized	wrath

1. **Little** acorns can grow into _____ oaks.

2. There was **ample** rain upstate, but here the precipitation was

_____ .

3. **Be quick in leaving**; don't _____ .

4. One of the sisters is a(n) _____ attorney; the other has had an **undistinguished** career.

5. Only two of the witnesses seemed _____ ; the rest were **unworthy of belief**.

6. You have made many _____ remarks about the candidates, but you haven't said one **complimentary** word about any of them.

7. When your dentist injects novocaine, the immediate area becomes _____ , but the rest of the mouth is **not deprived of feeling**.

8. The rebels **liberated** all the political prisoners that the ousted dictator had _____**ed**.

9. My _____ was aroused when I was over-charged, but after the manager apologized for the error, I had a feeling of **gratification**.

10. The building now has a(n) _____ exterior, but on the inside it is still **unostentatious**.

 CONCISE WRITING: Express the thought of each sentence in NO MORE THAN FOUR WORDS.

---

1. Those who have been found guilty of criminal offenses should be put behind prison bars.

   _____

2. Was the searching investigation that was conducted worth all the time, money, and effort that was put into it?

   _____

3. Did the alibi that she offered appear to be worthy of belief?

   _____

4. That narrow, small, exclusive group of people meets every day of the week.

   _____

5. Critics who write reviews are often the cause of bitter resentment in authors who are in the profession of writing plays.

   _____

6. Every one of us has experienced the mental distress that comes on the heels of failure or disappointment.

   _____

ANALOGIES: Which lettered pair of words—**a, b, c, d,** or **e**—most nearly has the same relationship as the numbered pair? Enter the letter of your answer in the space provided.

1. FLATTERER : CAJOLERY

   a. trespasser : law   *b.* perjurer : falsehood
   c. debtor : money   *d.* spendthrift : poverty
   e. alcoholic : restraint

1. _____

2. COTERIE : GROUP

   a. laugh : giggle   *b.* seat : stool
   c. smirk : smile   *d.* conversation : chat
   e. dinner : snack

   Hint: a COTERIE is a small GROUP.   2. _____

3. NUMB : SENSATION

   a. weary : fatigue   *b.* hoarse : irritation
   c. affluent : funds   *d.* apathetic : concern
   e. popular : friends

3. _____

4. ILLUSTRIOUS : INFAMOUS

   a. opulent : prosperous   *b.* enormous : huge
   c. significant : immaterial   *d.* inflexible : adamant
   e. precipitous : steep

4. _____

5. CRESTFALLEN : CHAGRIN

   a. altruistic : unkindness   *b.* rueful : joy
   c. obstinate : compromise   *d.* pallid : health
   e. hostile : antagonism

5. _____

6. PRODIGIOUS : STATURE

   a. mediocre : talent   *b.* powerless : influence
   c. zealous : enthusiasm   *d.* hesitant : confidence
   e. oafish : intelligence

6. _____

7. OSTENTATIOUS : IMPRESS

   a. counterfeit : deceive   *b.* vague : explain
   c. inequitable : spurn   *d.* fraudulent : expose
   e. unfeasible : attempt

7. _____

LESSON 10: REVIEW AND ENRICHMENT

 CLOSE READING: Read the following statements. Then answer questions 1–10.

STATEMENTS

Anyone foolish enough to make a comment about the size of Cyrano de Bergerac's nose was almost certain to be challenged by him to a duel.

The night before the Battle of Philippi, Brutus had a strong inner feeling that he would not survive.

The brontosaurus, one of the dinosaurs that formerly dominated the earth, was about sixty feet long and weighed about twenty tons.

Though told that it was madness to seek revenge on Moby Dick, the white whale that had maimed him, Captain Ahab remained determined to pursue the monster.

People regarded Benedict Arnold as a brave and talented military leader, but they changed their opinion of him when he betrayed his country to the enemy.

The alchemists have been thwarted since the Middle Ages in their search for a way to turn base metals into gold.

Everything was going well at a party of the gods and goddesses on Mount Olympus until Eris, the Goddess of Discord, arrived uninvited.

The Thirteen Colonies rebelled against England because they wanted to be free.

When Claggart falsely accused Billy Budd of plotting a mutiny, Billy hit him once, killing him instantly.

The French fleet played a key role in Washington's defeat of the British army at Yorktown in 1781.

QUESTIONS

1. Who thrived aeons ago? _____

2. Who was dealt a lethal blow? _____

3. Whose reputation plummeted? _____

4. Who was bolstered? _____

5. Who had a foreboding? _____

6. Who wanted to convert something? _____

7. Who was sensitive to derogatory remarks? _____

8. Who refused to be subjugated? _____

9. Who adamantly adhered to a purpose? _____

10. Who marred a festive occasion?_____

 CONCISE WRITING: Make the following composition more concise. The first paragraph has been rewritten as a model. Do similarly with the other paragraphs, trying to use no more than the number of words suggested.

Romeo Meets Juliet

The Montagues and the Capulets were two families with an abundance of wealth who lived in the city of Verona, and who had nothing but bitter hatred for each other. Every now and then, when they met on the streets of the city, there was a chance that swords might be drawn, and one or more members of the Montague family, or of the Capulet family, or of both families, might lose an arm, a leg, or the sight of an eye, or even be killed in a bloody fight. (*Cut to about 35 words.*)

The Montagues and Capulets, two affluent families of Verona, were bitter enemies. Occasionally, when they met on the streets, swords might be drawn, and one or more of them might be maimed or killed.

Romeo, who is a young man still in his teens, and the son of Lord Montague, believes himself to be in love with Rosaline. However, she remains distant in feeling and interest, and does not return his love. Learning that Rosaline has been invited to attend a masquerade party being given that very night by the Capulet family, Romeo is determined to go there, in the hope that he might see her. (*Cut to about 35 words.*)

_____

_____

_____

_____

_____

_____

That evening, as Romeo and his friend Mercutio, who are wearing masks, enter the palace of the Capulets, Romeo has a strong inner conviction of a coming misfortune. The instant he sees Juliet, Lord Capulet's beautiful daughter, who is not yet fourteen years of age, and she sees him, the two of them fall in love at first sight. However, Romeo is recognized by Juliet's cousin Tybalt, who has a temper that cannot be controlled. (*Cut to about 50 words.*)

_____

_____

_____

_____

_____

_____

_____

_____

The presence of Romeo causes bitter resentment in Tybalt; he calls for a servant to bring him his sword at once, so that he might kill the intruder. Fortunately, he is prevented from achieving this purpose by Lord Capulet, who does not want anything to happen that might detract from the perfectness of the evening. (*Cut to about 30 words.*)

_____

_____

_____

_____

_____

_____

_____

 CLOSE READING: Read the following statements. Then answer questions 11–20.

STATEMENTS

"Fish and visitors smell in three days" is one of the many old sayings that Benjamin Franklin quoted in his *Poor Richard's Almanac.*

President Theodore Roosevelt, too weak as a child to attend school, became world famous as an adult for his physical endurance.

The entrance to the underworld in Greek and Roman mythology was closely guarded by Cerberus, a three-headed dog.

In the 1970's, Oscars and a Pulitzer Prize in Music were awarded to Scott Joplin, composer of "Maple Leaf Rag," who had died in 1917 at the age of 49.

Without thinking of all the possible consequences, King Midas wished that everything he touched might turn to gold.

For his defiance of the Greek gods, Atlas was condemned forever to bear the world on his shoulders.

The voyage around the world that Ferdinand Magellan led in 1519 showed once and for all that the world is not flat.

When Lewis and Clark explored the Pacific Northwest in 1804–05, Sacagawea—accompanied by her baby—joined them as a guide and interpreter.

After serving as Vice-President from 1801 to 1805, Aaron Burr was three times tried for treason and three times acquitted.

By drugging the drinks of King Duncan's bodyguards, Lady Macbeth made it easier for Macbeth to murder the king.

QUESTIONS

11. Who sustained a prodigious burden? _____

12. Who was exculpated? _____

13. Who abetted a criminal? _____

14. Who used adages? _____

15. Who acquired legendary stamina? _____

16. Who apparently had scant recognition while alive? _____

17. Who was a consultant on a trek? _____

18. Who helped dispel an erroneous belief? _____

19. Who coveted wealth? _____

20. Who maintained surveillance? _____

D | **BRAINTEASERS:** Fill in the missing letters, as in 1 and 2, below.

---

1. Her story does not **j i be** with the facts.

2. We thanked our loyal fans for their **u n waver i n g** support.

3. A winning streak helped us **boo _ _ our** standing in the league.

4. Hearing screams, I went to see what the **_ _ _ _ motion** was about.

5. No sooner is a(n) **_ ad** established than another arrives to take its place.

6. Be on your guard; your opponent is very **_ raft _**.

7. Let them achieve their goals; don't **_ _ wart** them.

8. When she lost her job, she was **_ _ _ _ _ _ fallen**.

9. A mild spring day is a(n) **_ _ _ _ _ _ tune** time for planting.

10. Why don't you replace this **_ _ _ _ _ let _ equipment**?

11. Reinforcements arrived to help us **_ _ pulse** the invaders.

12. It is illegal to drive with a license that has **_ _ _ _ _ red**.

13. Conclusions must be based on fact, not **_ _ _ _ position**.

14. If your excuse is **_ _ edible**, people may believe it.

15. Duke Ellington was **_ _ _ _ own _ _** as a bandleader and composer.

16. Whether you come by car, train, or bus is **_ _ material**, as long as you arrive on time.

17. Imagine my **_ _ _ _ grin** when I struck out for the fourth time.

18. Why won't you **_ _ knowledge** that you were wrong?

19. Part of the sinking ship was already below the **_ _ _ face** of the sea.

20. An overdose may be **fat _ _**.

LESSON 11

 LESSON WORDS 1–10: Pronounce the word, spell it, study its meanings, and finish the sentence that follows it.

---

amass (*v.*) collect for oneself; pile up; **accumulate**; **gather**
ə-ˈmas

  1. (Scholars, Misers) _____ *amass* a wealth of knowledge.

apprehensive (*adj.*) fearful about something that might happen; **uneasy**; **anxious**
ˌap-ri-ˈhen(t)-siv

  2. We are *apprehensive* when we lead by a (scant, insurmountable) _____ margin.

deplete (*v.*) empty completely or partially; **drain**; **exhaust**; **lessen**
di-ˈplēt

  3. The long (dry, rainy) _____ spell has almost *depleted* our reservoirs.

enigma (*n.*) something puzzling or hard to explain; **mystery**; **riddle**; **puzzle**
i-ˈnig-mə

  4. To (a literate, an illiterate) _____ person, a book is an *enigma*.

fathom (*v.*) get to the bottom of; understand thoroughly; **interpret**; **penetrate**
ˈfath-əm

  5. It takes (luck, astuteness) _____ to *fathom* an opponent's strategy.

gullible (*adj.*) easily tricked or cheated; **credulous**; **naive**
ˈgəl-ə-bəl

  6. *Gullible* people rarely (do, question) _____ what they are told.

imminent (*adj.*) about to take place; at hand; **impending**; **threatening**; **near**
ˈim-ə-nənt

7. The jury has (ended, begun) _____
deliberations; a verdict is *imminent*.

increment (*n.*) something added; **increase**; **addition**; **raise**
iŋ-krə-mənt

8. I was hired at $195 a week, and now I make $220; I got a

($15, $25) _____ *increment*.

initial (*adj.*) occurring at the beginning; **first**; **introductory**
in-ʼish-əl

9. Sally settled for ice cream because there was no rice pud-

ding; (ice cream, rice pudding) _____
was her *initial* choice.

lavish (*adj.*) very generous in giving or spending; **prodigal**; **pro-**
ʼlav·ish   **fuse**; **unstinting**

10. A *lavish* hostess serves (tiny, large) _____
portions.

SENTENCE COMPLETION 1–10: Enter the required lesson
words.

---

1. Our club was so _____ in its spending the past two

months that it almost _____**d** the treasury.

2. The smile of Leonardo da Vinci's Mona Lisa remains a(n)

_____ despite the efforts of countless viewers to

_____ it.

3. P. T. Barnum, who once said, "A sucker is born every minute,"

knew that people are _____, and he used that

knowledge to _____ a fortune.

4. Since new employees can qualify for a(n) _____

every six months, by year's end they may be earning much more

than their _____ salary.

5. After the earthquake, many of the region's terrified inhabitants

were _____ that another quake was

_____ .

SYNONYM ROUNDUP 1–10: Each completed line should have three synonyms. Enter the missing letters.

---

1. acc __ m __ late   g __ ther   __ m __ ss

2. anx __ __ __ s   un __ __ sy   appre __ __ __ sive

3. cred __ lous   n __ ive   gull __ __ __ __

4. exh __ __ st   d __ pl __ te   __ rain

5. f __ rst   intr __ d __ ct __ ry   init __ __ l

6. int __ rpr __ t   p __ n __ trate   fath __ m

7. m __ stery   __ n __ gma   puz __ __ __

8. pr __ f __ se   l __ vish   prod __ g __ l

9. r __ __ se   __ __ crease   incr __ m __ nt

10. thr __ __ tening   im __ __ nent   __ __ pending

LESSON WORDS 11–20: Pronounce the word, spell it, study its meanings, and finish the sentence that follows it.

legible (*adj.*)   capable of being read; easy to read; **readable**; **de-**
'lej-ə-bəl   **cipherable**

> 11. A (scribbled, typed) _____ message is usually
>   *legible*.

melancholy (*adj.*)   in a gloomy state of mind; **sad**; **depressed**;
'mel-ən-ˌkäl-ē   **heavyhearted**

> 12. A (pickup, downturn) _____ in sales
>   makes merchants *melancholy*.

obligatory (*adj.*)   legally or morally binding; **mandatory**; **re-**
ə-'blig-ə-ˌtȯr-ē   **quired**

> 13. It is *obligatory* for drivers to carry (passengers, identifi-
>   cation) _____ .

ordeal (*n.*)   extremely difficult experience that tries one's charac-
ȯr-'dē(ə)l   ter or endurance; **trial**; **test**

> 14. Living through a (hurricane, sun-shower) _____
>   is an *ordeal*.

paltry (*adj.*)   of little or no value; **cheap**; **shoddy**; **trivial**; **pica-**
'pȯl-trē   **yune**

> 15. A few (raindrops, nosebleeds) _____
>   are a *paltry* excuse for absence.

stalemate (*n.*)   situation in which no action can be taken; **dead-**
'stā(ə)l-ˌmāt   **lock**; **tie**; **draw**

> 16. Casualties (soar, plummet) _____ during a
>   *stalemate* in hostilities.

tension (*n.*)   mental or emotional strain; **suspense**; **anxiety**;
'ten-chən   **stress**

> 17. *Tension* (mounts, abates) _____ as we ap-
>   proach a crisis.

unscrupulous (*adj.*)   acting without strict regard for what is
ˌən-'skrü-pyə-ləs   right; lacking in moral principles; **unprin-**
      cipled; **conscienceless**

18. *Unscrupulous* politicians are mainly concerned with their (personal, community's) _____ welfare.

vicinity (*n.*)   surrounding area or region; **neighborhood**; **local-**
və-'sin-ət-ē   **ity**

19. Residents in the *vicinity* of the (airport, library) _____ complain of noise pollution.

vivacious (*adj.*)   full of life and spirits; **lively**; **sprightly**; **active**
və-'vā-shəs

20. *Vivacious* children are not usually (noisy, quiet) _____ .

SENTENCE COMPLETION 11–20: Enter the required lesson words from D, above.

---

1. The _____ pearl buyers of La Paz tried to force Kino to sell his beautiful rare pearl for the _____ sum of 1500 pesos.

2. Driving to your new house in last night's storm was a(n) _____ because the roads were flooded, and it was too dark for street signs to be _____ .

3. The _____ among the residents subsided when the escaped murderer reported to be in their _____ was recaptured.

4. Many think it should be _____ for union and management, when they reach a(n) _____ , to submit their differences to arbitration.

5. Pam, one of my most _____ friends, has been

_____ ever since she lost her dog.

SYNONYM ROUNDUP 11–20: Each line, when completed, should have three words similar in meaning. Fill in the missing letters.

---

11. consc __ __ nceless   unprincip __ __ d   unscr __ p __ lous

12. m __ l __ nch __ ly   d __ pressed   heav __ hearted

13. d __ __ dlock   __ ie   st __ l __ mate

14. l __ vely   v __ v __ cious   spri __ __ tly

15. n __ __ ghborhood   v __ c __ n __ ty   l __ c __ lity

16. read __ ble   leg __ ble   __ __ cipherable

17. req __ __ red   obl __ g __ tory   m __ nd __ tory

18. __ tress   anx __ __ ty   t __ ns __ __ n

19. t __ st   tri __ l   __ __ deal

20. tri __ __ al   p __ ltry   p __ c __ yune

SYNONYMS: To avoid repetition, replace the boldfaced word or expression with a synonym from the vocabulary list below.

deplete	mandatory	depressed	initial	accumulate
trial	locality	uneasy	anxiety	comprehend

1. Unless you are in top condition, basketball will quickly **exhaust** your energy; it is an exhausting sport.

1. _____

2. Having to take five examinations in one day is a(n) **trying experience** that Pat hopes never to experience again.

2. _____

3. In the **first** match, you were the first to score.

3. _____

4. If you look tense when you visit a seriously ill patient, you will only add to the **tension** he is having about his health.

4. _____

5. At that restaurant, jackets and ties are **required** for gentlemen, but no one had ever warned Dan of this requirement.

5. _____

6. How did you ever manage to **amass** such a mass of junk?

6. _____

7. Neighbors say that a disturbed stray dog has been seen in this **neighborhood**.

7. _____

8. After our defeat, there was an atmosphere of gloom in the stands; all the fans were **in a gloomy frame of mind**.

8. _____

9. The performers were a bit **apprehensive** before curtain time, but the warmth of the audience soon dispelled their apprehension.

9. _____

10. Champollion was able to **interpret** the Egyptian hieroglyphics, a picture language that had defied interpretation.   10. _____

ANTONYMS: In the blank space in each sentence below, enter the word most nearly the antonym of the boldfaced word or words. Choose your antonyms from the following list.

---

credulous   sprightly   undecipherable   shoddy   prodigal
impending   increment   unprincipled   drain   enigma

1. In a drought, we must be extremely **sparing**, rather than _____ , in using water.

2. Not everyone received a(n) _____ ; some had to take a **cut in pay**.

3. Most of the faculty's signatures were **legible**, but one was _____ .

4. Though they seemed to be **acting with a strict regard for what is right and what is wrong**, they were really _____ .

5. Exaggerated advertising claims may mislead some _____ people, but not the **astute** shopper.

6. A person who is poor in explaining can make **something not puzzling** seem like a(n) _____ .

7. If we _____ our timber reserves, it will be hard to **replace** them.

8. These puppies are extremely _____ ; only when they are asleep are they **inactive**.

9. The necklace Matilda had lost was really not **valuable**; it was a(n) _____ imitation of an expensive necklace.

10. Before discussing problems that seem **far off in the future**, let us deal with some _____ issues.

CONCISE WRITING: Express the thought of each sentence in NO MORE THAN FOUR WORDS.

1. A work stoppage to force compliance with the employees' demands is about to take place.

   _____

2. A troubleshooter gets to the bottom of things that are puzzling or hard to explain.

   _____

3. The extremely difficult and trying experience that we have been going through is coming to an end.

   _____

4. Has there ever been a time when you were in a gloomy state of mind?

   _____

5. The person that you have allied yourself with does not seem to have a strict regard for what is right and proper.

   _____

6. Those who were new to the job were fearful that something might happen.

   _____

ANALOGIES: Which lettered pair of words—**a, b, c, d,** or **e**— most nearly has the same relationship as the numbered pair? Enter the letter of your answer in the space provided.

1. VICINITY : NEIGHBORHOOD

   _a._ blemish : perfection   _b._ probability : likelihood
   _c._ dearth : surplus   _d._ outskirts : distance
   _e._ capital : nation   1. _____

2. FOREBODING : TENSION

    a. caution : mishap   *b.* comedy : laughter
    c. boredom : repetition   *d.* warmth : sun
    e. inflexibility : compromise   2. _____

3. AMASS : DISTRIBUTE

    a. thrive : flourish   *b.* frustrate : thwart
    c. absolve : vindicate   *d.* encourage : deter
    e. encroach : trespass   3. _____

4. ENIGMATIC : UNDERSTAND

    a. simple : learn   *b.* feasible : accomplish
    c. delectable : consume   *d.* visible : notice
    e. rare : find   4. _____

5. MANDATORY : IGNORE

    a. defective : repair   *b.* obsolete : replace
    c. unjust : countenance   *d.* praiseworthy : commend
    e. inaccurate : correct   5. _____

6. PICAYUNE : INVALUABLE

    a. steep : sheer   *b.* final : conclusive
    c. expedient : advisable   *d.* opportune : favorable
    e. trite : fresh   6. _____

7. SPEND : PRODIGAL

    a. work : lazy   *b.* waste : thrifty
    c. care : indifferent   *d.* borrow : prudent
    e. talk : loquacious   7. _____

LESSON 12

LESSON WORDS 1–10: Pronounce the word, spell it, study its meanings, and finish the sentence that follows it.

adorn (*v.*)   add beauty to; make more attractive; **decorate**; **em-**
ə-ˈdo(ə)rn   **bellish**; **beautify**

   1. The room is beautiful; (cobwebs, paintings) _____ *adorn* the walls.

appalling (*adj.*)   filled with horror, shock, or dismay; **frightful**;
ə-ˈpȯl·iŋ   **shocking**

   2. There was (great, no) _____ suffering; conditions were *appalling*.

barren (*adj.*)   producing little or no vegetation; incapable of pro-
ˈbar·ən   ducing offspring; **unproductive**; **sterile**

   3. *Barren* fields yield (bumper, meager) _____ crops.

buffoon (*n.*)   person given to joking, clowning, or playing pranks;
(ˌ)bə-ˈfün   **clown**; **zany**

   4. The   circus   *buffoons*   make   children   (cry,   laugh) _____ .

congenial (*adj.*)   having   the   same   tastes   and   temperament;
kən-ˈjēn-yəl   **friendly**; **sociable**

   5. *Congenial* people (rarely, never) _____ disagree.

corroborate (*v.*)   support with evidence; **confirm**; **substanti-**
kə-ˈräb-ə-ˌrāt   **ate**; **verify**

   6. Rumor becomes truth (before, after) _____ it is *corroborated*.

curtail (*v.*)   cut back; **shorten**; **lessen**; **abbreviate**; **reduce**
(ˌ)kər-ˈtā(ə)l

    7. Service is *curtailed* today; (fewer, more) _____
       busses are running.

deplore (*v.*)   regret strongly; disapprove of; feel grief for; **lament**;
di-ˈplȯ(ə)r   **bewail**

    8. We *deplore* your conduct. Why were you (unkempt, un-

       civil) _____?

enhance (*v.*)   add or contribute to; **increase**; **augment**; **im-**
in-ˈhan(t)s   **prove**; **intensify**

    9. Spices *enhance* the (flavor, spoilage) _____ of
       food.

festive (*adj.*)   of or suited to a feast or festival; **joyful**; **merry**;
ˈfes-tiv   **jovial**

    10. On a *festive* occasion, let us not be (melancholy, merry)

       _____ .

 SENTENCE COMPLETION 1–10: Enter the required lesson words.

---

1. Both the North and the South deeply _____d the

    _____ bloodshed in the Battle of Gettysburg, in

    which 50,000 soldiers lost their lives.

2. Joke and clown, if you wish, at _____

    gatherings, like parties, but in an employment interview don't

    behave like a(n) _____ .

3. Though the charges that the candidate is an alcoholic have yet

to be _____**d**, they have certainly not

_____**d** his reputation.

4. Our neighbor Rose was going to _____ her visit to

the playground, but she changed her mind when her children

found _____ playmates there.

5. Here and there, a flowering cactus _____**s** the other-

wise _____ desert.

 SYNONYM ROUNDUP 1–10: Each completed line should have three synonyms. Enter the missing letters.

---

1. beaut __ fy   ad __ rn   __ __ bellish

2. b __ wail   l __ ment   d __ pl __ re

3. cl __ __ n   b __ ff __ __ n   z __ ny

4. __ __ __ firm   substant __ __ te   c __ rr __ b __ rate

5. congen __ __ l   fr __ __ ndly   soc __ __ ble

6. fri __ __ tful   sh __ cking   ap __ __ lling

7. incr __ __ se   a __ gment   enhan __ e

8. less __ n   curt __ __ l   red __ ce

9. j __ vial   joy __ __ l   f __ st __ ve

10. __ __ productive   b __ rren   st __ r __ le

LESSON WORDS 11–20: Pronounce the word, spell it, study its meanings, and finish the sentence that follows it.

---

malicious (*adj.*) full of malice (ill will); desirous of doing mischief
mə-'lish-əs   or making others suffer; **spiteful**; **malevolent**

11. A *malicious* fan pelted the visitors with (flowers, eggs)

_____ .

meritorious (*adj.*) worthy of honor; **praiseworthy**; **com-**
ˌmer-ə-tȯr-ē-əs   **mendable**; **laudable**; **deserving**

12. *Meritorious* deeds should not be (rewarded, ignored)

_____ .

minimize (*v.*) make (something or someone) appear as unimpor-
'min-ə-ˌmīz   tant as possible; **belittle**; **disparage**; **decry**

13. By boasting that she had done (nothing, everything)

_____ , she *minimized* our contribution
to the show.

obligation (*n.*) something one is bound to do; **duty**; **responsi-**
ˌäb-lə-'gā-shən **bility**

14. It is a tenant's *obligation* to (pay, collect) _____
rent.

preposterous (*adj.*) completely contrary to nature, reason, or
pri-'päs-t(ə-)rəs   common sense; utterly foolish; **absurd**;
    senseless; **ridiculous**

15. It is *preposterous* to claim to be (invincible, vulnerable)

_____ .

procrastinate (*v.*) defer action; habitually put off the doing of
p(r)ə-'kras-tə-ˌnāt something that should be done; **delay**; **daw-**
    dle; **postpone**

16. I was far (behind, ahead) _____ because I had
procrastinated.

reimburse (*v.*)   make repayment (to someone) for expenses or
‚re-əm-ˈbərs   losses incurred; **repay**; **recompense**; **compensate**

    17. Ann *reimbursed* me for the things I had (bought, sold)

        _____ for her.

skinflint (*n.*)   one who is very hard and grasping in money mat-
ˈskin-ˌflint   ters; **miser**; **tightwad**; **pinchpenny**

    18. *Skinflints*, as a rule, tip very (lavishly, sparingly)

        _____ .

toxic (*adj.*)   affected by or acting as a poison; **poisonous**; **venomous**
ˈtäk-sik

    19. The (honey, sting) _____ of a bee can have a *toxic*
        effect.

zeal (*n.*)   intense enthusiasm; impassioned eagerness; **ardor**; **fervor**; **passion**
ˈzē(ə)l

    20. I was (chided, praised) _____ for a lack of *zeal*
        in doing my chores.

 SENTENCE COMPLETION 11–20: Enter the required lesson words from D, above.

---

1. Donna was applauded for her acting by everyone except a(n)

    _____ rival who tried to _____

    her achievement.

2. Since Gulliver had just rendered highly _____

    service to the kingdom of Lilliput, it was _____

    that he should be accused of treason.

3. If you incur any expenses in doing Randy a favor, you may be sure he will quickly _____ you; he is no _____ .

4. Let us act now to stop the illegal dumping of _____ wastes; if we _____ , the situation will only get worse.

5. The rescue squad deserves praise for its speedy response in emergencies, and for the skill and _____ with which it performs its _____ s.

SYNONYM ROUNDUP 11–20: Each line, when completed, should have three words similar in meaning. Fill in the missing letters.

---

11. __ bsurd   prep__ st__ rous   r __ d __ culous

12. b __ little   m __ n __ mize   disp __ r __ ge

13. commend __ ble   l __ __ dable   m __ r __ torious

14. d __ lay   d __ wdle   procrast __ nate

15. d __ ty   obl __ gation   respons __ b __ l __ ty

16. f __ rv __ r   ard __ r   z __ __ l

17. m __ ser   t __ ghtw __ d   __ __ __ __ __ flint

18. p __ __ s __ nous   t __ xic   v __ n __ mous

19. re __ __ burse   c __ __ pensate   __ __ compense

20. sp __ teful   m __ lic __ __ us   mal __ v __ lent

SYNONYMS: To avoid repetition, replace the boldfaced word with a synonym from the vocabulary list below.

bewail	**poisonous**	**substantiate**	**jovial**	**frightful**
recompense	**spiteful**	**responsibility**	**ardor**	**laudable**

1. Lead, a highly **toxic** metal, was used extensively in water pipes in the olden days when its toxicity was unknown.

1. _____

2. Some say Joe's idea is **meritorious**, but I see no merit in it.

2. _____

3. We are appalled by the bad news; the situation is **appalling**.

3. _____

4. At first, we zealously supported our legislator, but when he was convicted of taking bribes, our **zeal** for him plummeted.

4. _____

5. Witnesses were called to **corroborate** the defendant's claim, but the scant evidence they offered fell far short of corroboration.

5. _____

6. Though some in the past have been **reimbursed** for their expenses, I have no assurance that I will receive any reimbursement.

6. _____**d**

7. Your fellow employees are not obliged to do your work for you; that is your **obligation**.

7. _____

8. Let's not **deplore** our fate; it is not so deplorable as we think.

8. _____

9. Although you insist that your coach is **malicious**, we see no malice in her whatsoever.

9. _____

10. People who attend a festival are usually in a **festive** mood.

10. _____

H **ANTONYMS:** In the blank in each sentence below, enter the word most nearly the antonym of the boldfaced word or words. Choose your antonyms from the following list.

**confirm augment   abbreviate absurd   sterile
sociable malevolent venomous embellish commendable**

1. Not all of the suggestions were **sensible**; a few were utterly

    _____.

2. Unlike garter snakes, which are **nonpoisonous**, rattlesnakes

    are dangerously _____.

3. Horses are **capable of producing offspring**, but mules are

    _____.

4. Graffiti **mar the appearance of** a wall; they surely do not

    _____ it.

5. Othello failed to see that Iago, who seemed like a person **of

    good will**, was in fact _____.

6. So far, there is little to **contradict** or _____
    the existence of other worlds like ours in the universe.

7. Our guests had intended to **extend** their visit, but inclement

    weather compelled them to _____ it.

8. By its conduct, a nation can either _____ or
    decrease its prestige.

9. Keisha reports that her colleagues in the office are quite

    _____, except for one or two who seem **un-
    congenial**.

10. Benedict Arnold must have been riled when his superiors con-
    sidered his outstandingly _____
    battlefield record **undeserving** of promotion.

 CONCISE WRITING: Express the thought of each sentence
in NO MORE THAN FOUR WORDS.

---

1. Why are you in the habit of putting off the doing of what has to
   be done now to some indefinite time in the future?

   _____

2. She makes the hardships that she has been going through seem
   as unimportant as possible.

   _____

3. In matters that have to do with money, he is very hard and grasping.

   _____

4. The stories that they have been telling are full of horror, shock,
   and dismay.

   _____

5. Stay away from those who are desirous of making other people
   suffer or doing mischief.

   _____

6. Do your teammates have the same temperament and tastes that
   you have?

   _____

ANALOGIES: Which lettered pair of words—**a, b, c, d,** or **e**— most nearly has the same relationship as the numbered pair? Enter the letter of your answer in the space provided.

1. ARSENIC : TOXICITY

    a. glass : durability   *b.* rubber : elasticity
    c. sound : visibility   *d.* ice : warmth
    e. blizzard : transportation   1. _____

2. HUMANE : MALICE

    a. energetic : vigor   *b.* zealous : enthusiasm
    c. timid : misgiving   *d.* unprejudiced : bias
    e. appreciative : gratitude   2. _____

3. PROCRASTINATOR : POSTPONE

    a. obstructionist : thwart   *b.* suspect : interrogate
    c. prisoner : incarcerate   *d.* bungler : excel
    e. monarch : obey   3. _____

4. FAN : ZEAL

    a. addict : self-control   *b.* pinchpenny : greed
    c. oaf : intelligence   *d.* botcher : aptitude
    e. holdout : contract   4. _____

5. PREPOSTEROUS : REASON

    a. complex : difficulty   *b.* appalling : horror
    c. erroneous : fact   *d.* injurious : harm
    e. deserving : merit   5. _____

6. DISPARAGE : PRAISE

    a. rue : deplore   *b.* prohibit : interdict
    c. deplete : replace   *d.* mar : impair
    e. verify : substantiate   6. _____

7. BUFFOONERY : AMUSEMENT

    a. medication : pain   *b.* collision : speeding
    c. virus : flu   *d.* unemployment : recession
    e. perspiration : heat   7. _____

LESSON 13

 LESSON WORDS 1–10: Pronounce the word, spell it, study its meanings, and finish the sentence that follows it.

---

allot (*v.*) give as a share or portion; **assign**; **allocate**; **apportion**
ə-'lät

    1. Since only twelve minutes were left, each of the three candidates was *allotted* (four, three) _____ minutes for a summary.

appropriate (*v.*) take without permission for one's own use;
ə-'prō-prē-ˌāt   **seize**; **annex**

    2. The law of the jungle (forbids, permits) _____ the strong to *appropriate* the property of the weak.

dialogue (*n.*) exchange of ideas; **conversation**; **discussion**;
'dī-ə-ˌläg   **chat**

    3. We (greeted, ignored) _____ each other; there was no *dialogue*.

dispensable (*adj.*) capable of being done without; **nonessen-**
dis-'pen(t)-sə-bəl   **tial**; **unimportant**

    4. In (nonsmoking, smoking) _____ areas, ashtrays are *dispensable*.

eliminate (*v.*) get rid of; **remove**; **exclude**
i-'lim-ə-ˌnāt

    5. If tolls are *eliminated*, traffic will (slow down, speed up) _____ .

entice (*v.*) lead on by exciting hope or desire; **tempt**; **lure**; **in-**
in-'tīs   **veigle**

    6. (Pleasant, Obnoxious) _____ odors *enticed* us into the kitchen.

expedite (v.) speed up the process of; **hasten**; **accelerate**
'ek-spə-ˌdīt

> 7. Order by (phone, mail) _____ to *expedite* delivery.

fracas (n.) noisy, disorderly disturbance or fight; **altercation**;
'frāk-əs   **brawl**; **row**

> 8. When we have no umpire, there is (more, less) _____ likelihood of a *fracas*.

frugal (adj.) avoiding waste; not spending unnecessarily; **sparing**; **economical**; **thrifty**
'frü-gəl

> 9. One has to be *frugal* to live on a (meager, generous) _____ income.

function (n.) action proper to a person or thing; **purpose**; **duty**;
'fəŋ(k)-shən   **role**

> 10. The *function* of a heater is to (lower, elevate) _____ the temperature.

B **SENTENCE COMPLETION 1–10:** Enter the required lesson words.

---

1. Gail's _____ at the department store is to

   _____ the application process for credit cards.

2. One way for the government to reduce expenses is to

   _____ all _____ items

   from next year's budget.

3. A latecomer's attempt to _____ someone's seat in the rear of the auditorium touched off a brief but heated _____ .

4. After surrounding his hideout, the police _____**d** the armed convict into a(n) _____ , and shortly afterward he surrendered peacefully.

5. Be _____ in serving the ice cream, or some of us may not get any; _____ no more than one scoop per person until everyone has been served.

 SYNONYM ROUNDUP 1–10: Each completed line should have three synonyms. Enter the missing letters.

---

1. rem __ ve	excl __ de	el __ m __ nate
2. p __ rpose	r __ le	fun __ tion
3. ass __ gn	all __ cate	all __ t
4. h __ st __ n	exp __ dite	ac __ __ lerate
5. nonessent __ __ l	__ __ important	disp __ ns __ ble
6. br __ wl	fr __ c __ s	alt __ rc __ tion
7. s __ __ ze	ann __ x	appropr __ __ te
8. l __ re	ent __ ce	inv __ __ gle
9. conv __ rs __ tion	disc __ ssion	di __ l __ gue
10. ec __ n __ mical	fr __ g __ l	__ __ rifty

LESSON WORDS 11–20: Pronounce the word, spell it, study its meanings, and finish the sentence that follows it.

irate (*adj.*)   arising from or characterized by anger; **enraged**; **fu-**
ī-ˈrāt   **rious**

   11. His *irate* reply shows he was (puzzled, offended)
   _____ by her question.

lackluster (*adj.*)   lacking brilliance or vitality; **dull**; **uninspired**;
ˈlak-ˌləs-tər   **mediocre**

   12. Merchants are (impressed, unhappy) _____
   with *lackluster* profits.

mimic (*n.*)   one who mimics or imitates; **imitator**; **impersona-**
ˈmim-ik   **tor**

   13. Some *mimics* excel in (imitating, correcting) _____
   the speech of celebrities.

omnipotent (*adj.*)   having unlimited or very great power or au-
äm-ˈnip-ət-ənt   thority; **all-powerful**; **almighty**

   14. The Greeks knew there was (a, no) _____ limit to what
   they could do, but they considered their gods *omnipotent*.

quandary (*n.*)   state of uncertainty as to what to do: **dilemma**;
ˈkwän-d(ə-)rē   **predicament**

   15. Experts who give (conflicting, detailed) _____
   advice put us in a *quandary*.

ravenous (*adj.*)   extremely eager for food; **famished**; **voracious**
ˈrav-(ə-)nəs

   16. The *ravenous* guests devoured everything but the (ripe,
   artificial) _____ fruit.

slacken (*v.*)   make less active; slow up; **relax**; **untighten**; **mod-**
'slak-ən   **erate**

17. Accidents (rise, decline) _____ when the en-
forcement of traffic rules is *slackened.*

unnerve (*v.*)   cause to lose courage or confidence; **upset**; **fluster**;
ˌən-'nərv   **disconcert**

18. The shouts of hostile fans so *unnerved* Paula that she
(scored, missed) _____ an easy basket.

urgent (*adj.*)   requiring immediate attention; **pressing**; **compel-**
'ər-jənt   **ling**; **grave**

19. When reservoirs are nearly (empty, full) _____,
there is *urgent* need for conservation.

vulnerable (*adj.*)   open to attack, injury, or damage; **assailable**;
'vəln-(ə-)rə-bəl   **exposed**

20. If streams overflow, homes on (high, low) _____
ground may be *vulnerable* to flooding.

SENTENCE COMPLETION 11–20: Enter the required lesson words from D, above.

---

1. The plight of the earthquake survivors is so _____

that we must not _____ our efforts to help them.

2. It is a dangerous mistake for champions to think they are

_____; overconfidence may make them

_____ .

3. Who would not be _____d on an Arctic night to

hear the howls of _____ wolves getting closer

and closer?

4. The director was so _____ over the band's

_____ performance that she scheduled an

extra rehearsal for the next day.

5. You would be in a(n) _____ if you tried to identify

the mockingbird by its song because it is a gifted

_____ of other birds.

SYNONYM ROUNDUP 11–20: Each line, when completed, should have three words similar in meaning. Enter the missing letters.

---

11. pr __ ssing   __ rg __ nt   gr __ ve

12. __ __ nerve   fl __ ster   d __ __ concert

13. im __ tat __ r   m __ m __ c   __ __ personator

14. fur __ __ us   enr __ ged   __ rate

15. rel __ x   __ __ tighten   sl __ ck __ n

16. all-p __ w __ rful   omn __ p __ tent   __ __ mighty

17. f __ mished   v __ r __ cious   r __ v __ nous

18. l __ ckl __ ster   un __ __ spired   med __ __ cre

19. ass __ __ lable   exp __ sed   v __ ln __ r __ ble

20. qu __ nd __ ry   d __ lemma   pr __ d __ c __ ment

SYNONYMS: To avoid repetition, replace the boldfaced word or expression with a synonym from the vocabulary list below.

inveigle	seize	economical	disconcert	enraged
pressing	relax	uninspiring	nonessential	dilemma

1. If the decorations are **dispensable**, let's dispense with them.

1. _____

2. It is inappropriate for anyone to **appropriate** vacant property.

2. _____

3. Your grip on the bat is too tight; **untighten** it a bit.

3. _____

4. Some people are uncertain about so many things that they are always in a(n) **state of uncertainty**.

4. _____

5. Parking is truly a(n) **urgent** matter, but there are problems of much greater urgency confronting us.

5. _____

6. A nervous person is easily **unnerved** by an unexpected change.

6. _____**ed**

7. Critics look for excellence, not mediocrity; they steer the public away from **mediocre** productions.

7. _____

8. The misleading offer was so enticing that many were **enticed** into accepting it.

8. _____**d**

9. When our health is at risk, we spare no expense to get well; otherwise, we are **sparing** with our money.

9. _____

10. The captain would become **furious** when his ire was aroused, so the crew tried not to infuriate him.

10. _____

ANTONYMS: In the blank space in each sentence below, enter the word most nearly the antonym of the boldfaced word or words. Choose your antonyms from the following list.

unassailable	moderate	inspired	appropriate	calm
indispensable	lavish	restore	powerless	repel

1. The defendants had been _____ during the trial, but when they heard the verdict, they became **irate**.

2. Does violence in a movie _____ you, or does it **lure** you to keep watching?

3. The castle was _____, but the rest of the place was **open to attack**.

4. With limited resources, we must be **frugal**; we cannot afford to be _____.

5. In totalitarian states, rulers are **omnipotent** and subjects are

   _____.

6. Don't expect an actress to give a(n) _____ performance if she has to work with a **dull** script.

7. Some want us to **speed up** our pace; others say we should

   _____ it.

8. Leave **nonessential** equipment behind; take along only what is _____.

9. None of the items **eliminated** from the budget have been

   _____**d**.

10. Did he **take** your bicycle **with permission**, or did he simply

    _____ it?

CONCISE WRITING: Express the thought of each sentence in NO MORE THAN FOUR WORDS.

1. All of a sudden, the exchange of ideas that they had been having came to an abrupt end.

    _____

2. Who is the individual who started that noisy, disorderly disturbance?

    _____

3. The situation that we find ourselves in is one that requires immediate attention.

    _____

4. There seemed to be no limit whatsoever to the power of the invaders.

    _____

5. Someone took the racket that belongs to Cynthia without bothering to ask her permission.

    _____

6. The boos that were emitted caused us to lose confidence in ourselves.

    _____

 ANALOGIES: Which lettered pair of words—**a, b, c, d**, or **e**—most nearly has the same relationship as the numbered pair? Enter the letter of your answer in the space provided.

1. GULLIBLE : ENTICE

        a. conspicuous : ignore   *b.* invincible : subdue
        c. unprincipled : bribe   *d.* adamant : persuade
        e. elusive : apprehend   1. _____

2. EFFICIENT : EXPEDITE

        a. greedy : share   *b.* gossipy : advertise
        c. dissenting : agree   *d.* thrifty : waste
        e. proficient : botch   2. _____

3. LACKLUSTER : BRILLIANCE

    a. invaluable : value   *b.* significant : meaning
    c. permanent : endurance   *d.* unadorned : embellishment
    e. toxic : poison   3. _____

4. OMNIPOTENT : AUTHORITY

    a. opulent : means   *b.* apprehensive : confidence
    c. malicious : goodness   *d.* negligent : reliability
    e. unscrupulous : honesty   4. _____

5. VULNERABLE : PROTECT

    a. mediocre : applaud   *b.* defective : repair
    c. trite : repeat   *d.* meritorious : belittle
    e. obvious : explain   5. _____

6. QUANDARY : PERPLEXED

    a. nap : awake   *b.* rut : progressing
    c. prison : free   *d.* clique : aloof
    e. race : unopposed   6. _____

7. PARROT : MIMIC

    a. elephant : trunk   *b.* lion : den
    c. dog : companion   *d.* camel : hump
    e. bird : nest   7. _____

LESSON 14

affection (*n.*)   liking or attachment for a person or thing; **fond-**
ə-ˈfek-shən   **ness; devotion**

    1. My *affection* for the dog kept me from (stroking, striking)

    _____ it.

anticipate (*v.*)   give advance thought or treatment to; **expect;**
an-ˈtis-ə-ˌpāt   **foresee**

    2. Let's get to the game (five, thirty) _____
    minutes early because I *anticipate* trouble in finding a
    parking space.

coerce (*v.*)   force without regard for one's wishes; **compel; con-**
kō-ˈərs   **strain**

    3. We were not *coerced*; we signed (involuntarily, willingly)

    _____ .

copious (*adj.*)   large in quantity or number; **abundant; plenti-**
ˈkō-pē-əs   **ful; ample**

    4. Potato prices (soar, plummet) _____ when
    there is a *copious* supply.

dismal (*adj.*)   showing or causing gloom or misery; **dreary;**
ˈdiz-məl   **cheerless**

    5. Our spirits were (depressed, lifted) _____
    by the *dismal* weather.

dominant (*adj.*)   conspicuously   prominent;   **commanding;**
ˈdäm(-ə)-nənt   **preeminent; outstanding**

    6. The *dominant* team in the league has not (lost, won)

    _____ a game.

effect (*n.*)   something traceable to a cause; **result**; **consequence**;
i-'fekt   **outcome**

> 7. One *effect* of heavy rains is (higher, lower) _____ reservoir levels.

intent (*n.*)   state of mind with which something is done; **purpose**;
in-'tent   **design**; **aim**

> 8. Murder committed (with, without) _____ *intent* cannot be considered accidental.

jeopardize (*v.*)   put in jeopardy (danger); **endanger**; **imperil**;
'jep-ər-ˌdīz   **compromise**

> 9. Our (lavish, frugal) _____ use of natural resources *jeopardizes* the welfare of future generations.

laborious (*adj.*)   involving much hard work; **arduous**; **difficult**;
lə-'bȯr-ē-əs   **strenuous**

> 10. Computers make record keeping (more, less) _____ *laborious*.

SENTENCE COMPLETION 1–10: Enter the required lesson words.

---

1. The team's _____ record of two wins in its last eleven

   games _____**s** its chances of getting into the

   play-offs.

2. By _____ effort, country folk are able to

   amass a(n) _____ supply of firewood for the winter.

3. When sports stars who are friends compete against each other,

   all _____ between them is usually sup-

   pressed; winning is the _____ concern.

4. It was certainly not the manager's _____ to help the

   robbers; they _____**d** him into opening the safe.

5. When Midas begged the gods that everything he touched might

   turn to gold, he did not _____ the

   _____ this would have on his ability to eat.

 SYNONYM ROUNDUP 1–10: Each completed line should have three synonyms. Enter the missing letters.

---

1. ab __ nd __ nt	plent __ ful	c __ p __ ous
2. p __ rpose	int __ nt	d __ s __ gn
3. aff __ ction	d __ v __ tion	f __ ndness
4. imp __ r __ l	c __ mpr __ mise	j __ __ pardize
5. dr __ __ ry	ch __ __ rless	d __ sm __ l
6. res __ lt	eff __ ct	c __ ns __ quence
7. c __ mp __ l	constr __ __ n	c __ __ rce
8. l __ b __ rious	ard __ ous	str __ n __ ous
9. exp __ ct	for __ see	ant __ c __ pate
10. c __ mm __ nding	d __ min __ nt	pr __ __ minent

 LESSON WORDS 11–20: Pronounce the word, spell it, study its meanings, and finish the sentence that follows it.

---

opinionated (*adj.*)   holding unreasonably to one's own opinions or
ə-ˈpin-yə-ˌnāt-əd   to   preconceived   notions;   **prejudiced**;
                         biased; **stubborn**

   11. *Opinionated* persons are (loath, prone) _____ to
       modify their views.

option (*n.*)   power or right of choosing; something that may be or
ˈäp-shən   is chosen; **choice**; **selection**

    12. If a sale is marked "final," the customer (loses, gets)

      _____ the *option* of returning the merchandise
      for a refund.

outlandish (*adj.*)   very odd; **strange**; **peculiar**; **bizarre**
(ˈ)auṫ-ˈlan-dish

    13. Their *outlandish* manners are sure to (escape, gain)

      _____ notice.

pact (*n.*)   agreement between persons or nations; **compact**; **cov-**
ˈpakt   **enant**; **treaty**

    14. *Pacts* between (congenial, distrustful) _____
      neighbors tend to endure.

prompt (*v.*)   cause (someone) to do something; **incite**; **spur**;
ˈpräm(p)t   **induce**

    15. Poor reviews of a film *prompt* moviegoers to (view, shun)

      _____ it.

refute (*v.*)   prove to be erroneous; **contradict**; **disprove**; **rebut**
ri-ˈfyüt

    16. (Hearsay, Fact) _____ cannot be *refuted*.

repast (*n.*)   food and drink; **meal**; **dinner**; **feast**
ri-ˈpast

    17. The Thanksgiving *repast* consisted of seven (pages,

      courses) _____ .

tactful (*adj.*)   having a keen sense of what to say or do to maintain
ˈtakt-fəl   good will and avoid giving offense; **adroit**; **clever**;
      diplomatic

    18. (Ambassadors, Goalies) _____ are not ex-
      pected to be *tactful*.

vain (*adj.*)   of no avail; **useless**; **futile**; **unproductive**
ˈvān

> 19. It is *vain* for us to think we are (vulnerable, omnipotent)
>
> _____ .

vivid (*adj.*)   presenting the appearance of life; **lively**; **colorful**;
ˈviv-əd   **graphic**

> 20. The fruit in the painting is so *vivid* that it looks (artificial,
>
> edible) _____ .

 SENTENCE COMPLETION 11–20: Enter the required lesson words from D, above.

---

1. Audrey is confident that by being _____ she can

   _____ Oscar's arguments without hurting his feel-

   ings.

2. I have keenly _____ memories of the truly delicious

   _____s Grandma used to serve when we visited her.

3. At a Halloween party, you can appear in the most

   _____ costume, with no possibility that it

   will _____ people to question your sanity.

4. The employees have two _____s: either to accept the

   _____ the mediators have proposed, or to go on strike.

5. Our attempts to reason with your _____ cou-

   sin proved _____; we got nowhere.

SYNONYM ROUNDUP 11–20: Each line, when completed, should have three words similar in meaning. Enter the missing letters.

11. co __ tr __ dict   reb __ t   r __ f __ te

12. t __ ctf __ l   adr __ __ t   d __ pl __ matic

13. m __ __ l   r __ p __ st   f __ __ st

14. ch __ __ ce   s __ l __ ction   __ ption

15. pr __ mpt   sp __ r   inc __ te

16. st __ bb __ rn   pr __ j __ diced   op __ n __ __ nated

17. v __ __ n   __ __ productive   f __ t __ le

18. outl __ ndish   pec __ liar   b __ z __ rre

19. p __ ct   tr __ __ ty   c __ v __ n __ nt

20. v __ v __ d   c __ l __ rful   gr __ ph __ c

SYNONYMS: To avoid repetition, replace the boldfaced word with a synonym from the vocabulary list below.

bizarre   prejudiced covenant   graphic compromise
constrain diplomatic preeminent refute   design

1. The business decline has put the company into a dangerous financial position and **endangered** the future of its employees.

2. Learn to be **tactful**; avoid making tactless remarks.

3. She did not embarrass us intentionally; that was not her **intent**.

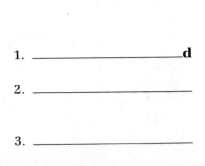

1. _____ d

2. _____

3. _____

4. Her **lively** details made the incident come to life.

4. _____

5. In the rebuttal, debaters have a chance to **rebut** their opponents' arguments.

5. _____

6. When he is wrong about a person, he alters his opinion; he is not **opinionated**.

6. _____

7. Shakespeare was the **dominant** literary figure of his time; he dominated the era.

7. _____

8. What a strange excuse! I never have heard of anything so **strange**.

8. _____

9. There was no compulsion; no one was **compelled** to contribute.

9. _____**ed**

10. Most observers agree that some of those who signed the **agreement** are not living up to its terms.

10. _____

 ANTONYMS: In the blank space in each sentence below, enter the word most nearly the antonym of the boldfaced word or words. Choose your antonyms from the following list.

---

spur	option	productive	everyday	coldness
expect	malevolent	scarce	effortless	cheerful

1. In spite of the depressingly **dismal** outlook, they seemed

_____ .

2. Before, we had absolutely **no choice** at all; now we have a(n) _____ .

3. Sometimes a tactless remark can turn **affection** into

_____ .

4. The Wooden Horse seemed to the Trojans like a gift **with good intent**, but those who were making the gift were, of course,

_____ .

5. Huge jackpots _____ some to buy lottery tickets, but they **do not induce** others to part with a penny.

6. Putting aside our _____ clothes, we donned **outlandish** costumes for the masquerade.

7. You _____ed her party to be a success; we **did not anticipate** it.

8. With the proper tools, a **laborious** task can be almost

_____ .

9. Job opportunities are **abundant** in good times but

_____ in a depression.

10. Their attempts to solve the enigma were

_____ , but mine proved **futile**.

CONCISE WRITING: Express the thought of each sentence in NO MORE THAN FOUR WORDS.

---

1. Janet proved that the statement that you made was in error.

   _____

2. In spite of all logic and reason, Tom held firmly to his own preconceived ideas and opinions.

   _____

3. The person who advises them has a keen sense of what to say and do to maintain good will and to avoid giving offense.

   _____

4. The attempts that I made turned out to be of no avail.

   _____

5. We gave advance thought to the problems that we would face.

   _____

6. The small routine jobs that have to be done on a farm involve a great deal of hard work.

   _____

ANALOGIES: Which lettered pair of words—**a, b, c, d,** or **e**—most nearly has the same relationship as the numbered pair? Enter the letter of your answer in the space provided.

1. IRREFUTABLE : DISPROVE

    a. foreseeable : anticipate   *b.* dispensable : omit
    c. inevitable : avoid   *d.* insignificant : ignore
    e. immaterial : disregard

        1. _____

2. JEOPARDY : SAFETY

    a. candor : honesty   *b.* proficiency : competence
    c. scarcity : dearth   *d.* insolence : respect
    e. vulnerability : exposure

        2. _____

3. REPAST : HUNGER

    a. infection : fever   *b.* increment : salary
    c. nap : fatigue   *d.* ordeal : tension
    e. uncertainty : anxiety

        3. _____

4. OPINIONATED : FLEXIBILITY

    a. indifferent : concern   *b.* charitable : generosity
    c. ardent : zeal   *d.* apprehensive : fear
    e. malicious : spite

        4. _____

5. VIVID : ALIVENESS

    a. unfathomable : solution   *b.* perfect : flaw
    c. bizarre : strangeness   *d.* turbulent : calmness
    e. unfounded : basis

        5. _____

6. PACT : AGREEMENT

    a. fish : ocean   *b.* container : jar
    c. vehicle : wheel   *d.* broccoli : vegetable
    e. periodical : magazine

        6. _____

7. DOMINANT : PREVAIL

    a. persistent : quit   *b.* adept : bungle
    c. naive : trust   *d.* economical : squander
    e. indefatigable : tire

        7. _____

LESSON 15: REVIEW AND ENRICHMENT

CLOSE READING: Read the following statements. Then answer questions 1–10.

STATEMENTS

Anyone in the seventeenth century who rented a horse from Hobson's stable had to take the one nearest to the door, like it or not.

Dunstan Cass, younger son of the wealthy Squire Cass, broke into Silas Marner's cottage and made off with a bag of gold.

Young David Copperfield could not get along with Mr. Murdstone, his hardhearted stepfather, who made life miserable for him.

Lisa's first words when she came home from the game were: "Is there anything to eat in this house? What's in the refrigerator? When will dinner be ready?"

When Neil Armstrong set foot on the moon on July 20, 1969, he saw nothing but stones, boulders, and craters.

In the first act of *Romeo and Juliet*, peace officers armed with clubs break up a fight between the Montagues and the Capulets on the streets of Verona.

Since the storm was moving rapidly up the coast, the authorities urged residents in low-lying areas to evacuate promptly to higher ground.

As a pioneer on the Dakota prairie, Per Hansa faced many hardships, but he was very enthusiastic about living there.

The strangers decided to go for a swim in the rough surf, scoffing at a sign on the beach that warned, "No lifeguards on duty."

When Terry left her office after work, the winds that had blown so violently in the morning had to her surprise become quite gentle.

QUESTIONS

1. Who seemed ravenous? _____

2. Who took part in a fracas? _____

3. Who appropriated something? _____

4. Who gave no options? _____

5. Who were judged to be vulnerable? _____

6. Who had to put up with someone uncongenial? _____

7. Who noticed a slackening? _____

8. Who showed zeal for something? _____

9. Who defiantly put themselves in jeopardy? _____

10. Who explored an apparently barren place? _____

 CONCISE WRITING: Cut the following 180-word editorial to no more than 130 words, without discarding any of its ideas.

The water supply problem has many of our city officials in a state of uncertainty as to what to do. No sooner does one water emergency pass than another seems about to occur. The problem is obviously one that requires immediate attention. Yet some politicians, especially those who like to put off what has to be done to some indefinite time in the future, try to make the problem seem as unimportant as possible. They argue that it will probably solve itself and that we should do nothing about it. But that seems completely contrary to all reason and common sense. We must not wait until our reservoirs are completely empty before taking action. Do we want to go through the same very difficult and trying experiences that many water-starved communities are now suffering?

One promising idea that is now being considered in other places is to speed up the process of installing water meters in every apartment and home. If they have to pay for their water, those people who are now very generous in its use may change their ways.

C

CLOSE READING: Read the following statements. Then answer questions 11–20.

STATEMENTS

In 1941, two years after negotiating a nonaggression treaty with Stalin, Hitler launched a massive surprise offensive against the Soviet Union.

"This is the last you will see of me," said the customer, storming out the door. "I will never shop here again."

Though the Etruscans controlled much of Italy for centuries before the Romans appeared, no one knows where they and their strange language came from.

After losing her title, the ex-champion was too depressed to talk with reporters.

In 1626, Peter Minuit gave the Native Americans who lived in Manhattan the equivalent of $24 in trinkets for the title to their property.

With the score tied at 2–2, the umpires called the opening game after six innings because of rain.

In "*The Deserted Village*," Oliver Goldsmith wrote: "In arguing, too, the parson showed his skill, For even though vanquished, he could argue still."

Tenants returning from shopping were surprised to find that the elevators were not running.

If the Royals had played without Stella, they would not have been able to win.

The new executive saved the company many millions by eliminating wasteful practices.

QUESTIONS

11. Who provided frugal management? _____

12. Who did not anticipate a mechanical breakdown? _____

13. Who was irate? _____

14. Who received seemingly paltry compensation? _____

15. Who broke a pact? _____

16. Who was melancholy? _____

17. Who seemed opinionated? _____

18. Who was indispensable? _____

19. Who curtailed something? _____

20. Who are an enigma? _____

 BRAINTEASERS: Fill in the missing letters, as in 1, below.

1. We had a nourishing and delicious <u>r</u> <u>e</u> **past**.

2. You won't have to work hard; the job is not too **labor** _ _ _ _.

3. Some still do not realize the _ _ _ _ **sequences** of smoking.

4. The low prices in the window are intended to _ _ _ _ **ice** customers.

5. Limited monarchs have little power, but dictators are _ _ **nip** _ _ _ _ _ _.

6. She deserves the promotion; her record is exceptionally **merit** _ _ _ _ _ _ _.

7. Investigators were shocked by the _ _ **pall** _ _ _ conditions they saw.

8. Swindlers are always on the lookout for **gull** _ _ _ _ _ victims.

9. The treasurer had to preside, though that is not her normal **fun** _ _ _ _ _.

10. They surrendered because further resistance would have been _ _ **tile**.

11. We passed each other silently; there was no **dial** _ _ _ _ between us.

12. Trapped in the elevator, they sang songs to ease the **ten** _ _ _ _.

13. The _ _ **tent** of the voyage was to find a shorter route to the Orient.

14. Critics were unimpressed by the cast's _ _ _ _ _ **luster** performance.

15. Why are you _ _ _ **concert** _ _? Is something upsetting you?

16. I don't have far to go to get home, since I live in the _ _ _ **in** _ _ _.

17. We do not approve of what has been done; we _ _ _ _ **lore** it.

18. That _ _ _ _ _ **penny** won't undertake to do anything that may cost money.

19. Her statement is absolutely true; no one can _ _ **but** it.

20. There was a(n) _ _ **pious** supply of cake a moment ago. It's all gone now.

Vocabulary Index

bold type = lesson word; light type = synonym

Pronunciation Symbols

ə   b**a**n**a**na, c**o**llide, ab**u**t

ˈə, ˌə   h**u**mdr**u**m, ab**u**t

ᵊ   immediately preceding \l\, \n\, \m\, \ŋ\, as in batt**le**, mitt**en**, eat**en**, and sometimes cap **an**d bells \-ᵊm-\, lock **an**d key \-ᵊŋ-\; immediately following \l\, \m\, \r\, as often in French tab**le**, pris**me**, tit**re**

ər   op**er**ation, f**ur**ther, **ur**g**er**

ˈər-   }

ˈə-r   }   as in two different pronunciations of h**urr**y \ˈhər-ē, ˈhə-rē\

a   m**a**t, m**a**p, m**a**d, g**a**g, sn**a**p, p**a**tch

ā   d**ay**, f**a**de, d**a**te, **a**orta, dr**a**pe, c**a**pe

ä   b**o**ther, c**o**t, and, with most American speakers, f**a**ther, c**a**rt

ȧ   f**a**ther as pronounced by speakers who do not rhyme it with b**o**ther

au̇   n**ow**, l**ou**d, **ou**t

b   **b**a**b**y, ri**b**

ch   **ch**in, nature \ˈnā-**ch**ər\ (actually, this sound is \t\ + \sh\)

d   **d**i**d**, a**dd**er

e   b**e**t, b**e**d, p**e**ck

ˈē, ˌē   b**ea**t, nos**e**bl**ee**d, **e**venly, **ea**sy

ē   eas**y**, meal**y**

f   **f**i**f**ty, cu**ff**

g   **g**o, bi**g**, **g**ift

h   **h**at, a**h**ead

hw   **wh**ale as pronounced by those who do not have the same pronunciation for both *whale* and *wail*

i   t**i**p, b**a**nish, act**i**ve

ī   s**i**te, s**i**de, b**uy**, tr**i**pe (actually, this sound is \ä\ + \i\, or \ȧ\ + \i\)

j   **j**ob, **g**em, e**dge**, **j**oin, **j**u**dge** (actually, this sound is \d\ + \zh\)

k   **k**in, **c**oo**k**, a**ch**e

k̲   German i**ch**, Bu**ch**

l   **l**i**l**y, poo**l**

m   **m**ur**m**ur, di**m**, ny**m**ph

n   **n**o, ow**n**

ⁿ   indicates that a preceding vowel or diphthong is pronounced with the nasal passages open, as in French *un bon vin blanc* \oeⁿ-bōⁿ-vaⁿ-bläⁿ\

ŋ sing \'siŋ\, singer \'siŋ-ər\, finger \'fiŋ-gər\, ink \'iŋk\

ō bone, know, beau

ȯ saw, all, gnaw

œ French bœuf, German Hölle

ō̄e French feu, German Höhle

ȯi coin, destroy, sawing

p pepper, lip

r red, car, rarity

s source, less

sh with nothing between, as in shy, mission, machine, special (actually, this is a single sound, not two); with a hyphen between, two sounds as in death's-head \'deths-ˌhed\

t tie, attack

th with nothing between, as in thin, ether (actually, this is a single sound, not two); with a hyphen between, two sounds as in knighthood \'nīt-ˌhu̇d\

t͟h then, either, this (actually, this is a single sound, not two)

ü rule, youth, union \'yün-yən\, few \'fyü\

u̇ pull, wood, book, curable \'kyu̇r-ə-bəl\

ue German füllen, hübsch

ūe French rue, German fühlen

v vivid, give

w we, away; in some words having final \(ˌ)ō\ a variant \ə-w\ occurs before vowels, as in \'fäl-ə-wiŋ\, covered by the variant \ə(-w)\ at the entry word

y yard, young, cue \'kyü\, union \'yün-yən\

ʸ indicates that during the articulation of the sound represented by the preceding character the front of the tongue has substantially the position it has for the articulation of the first sound of yard, as in French digne \dēnʸ\

yü youth, union, cue, few, mute

yu̇ curable, fury

z zone, raise

zh with nothing between, as in vision, azure \'azh-ər\ (actually, this is a single sound, not two); with a hyphen between, two sounds as in gazehound \'gāz-ˌhau̇nd\

\ slant line used in pairs to mark the beginning and end of a transcription: \'pen\

ˈ mark preceding a syllable with primary (strongest) stress: \'pen-mən-ˌship\

ˌ mark preceding a syllable with secondary (next-strongest) stress: \'pen-mən-ˌship\

- mark of syllable division

( ) indicate that what is symbolized between is present in some utterances but not in others: factory \'fak-t(ə)rē\